'The reasonable man adapts himself to the world. The unreasonable one persists in trying to adapt the world to himself. Therefore all progress depends on the unreasonable man.'

Man and Superman
George Bernard Shaw

'The great man understands the essence of a problem; the ordinary leader grasps only the symptoms.'

Years of Upheaval
Henry Kissinger

Copyright © 2023 Leslie Turnberg

The moral right of the author has been asserted.

Apart from any fair dealing for the purposes of research or private study, or criticism or review, as permitted under the Copyright, Designs and Patents Act 1988, this publication may only be reproduced, stored or transmitted, in any form or by any means, with the prior permission in writing of the publishers, or in the case of reprographic reproduction in accordance with the terms of licences issued by the Copyright Licensing Agency. Enquiries concerning reproduction outside those terms should be sent to the publishers.

Matador
Unit E2 Airfield Business Park,
Harrison Road, Market Harborough,
Leicestershire. LE16 7UL
Tel: 0116 2792299
Email: books@troubador.co.uk
Web: www.troubador.co.uk/matador
Twitter: @matadorbooks

ISBN 978 1805140 634

British Library Cataloguing in Publication Data.
A catalogue record for this book is available from the British Library.

Typeset in 13pt Baskerville by Troubador Publishing Ltd, Leicester, UK

Matador is an imprint of Troubador Publishing Ltd

An Unreasonable Man

Pinchas Rutenberg
The Russian revolutionary
who electrified Palestine

Leslie Turnberg

Contents

Acknowledgments		6
Preface		8
Introduction		11
Chapter 1	The lights go on in Allenby Street	16
Chapter 2	A revolutionary is born	20
Chapter 3	1905, Revolution	26
Chapter 4	Assassination	35
Chapter 5	Escape to Italy	43
Chapter 6	In America	50
Chapter 7	Russia beckons, 1917	62
Chapter 8	Grand electrical plans	68
Chapter 9	Facing the opposition	80
Chapter 10	Government antagonism	89
Chapter 11	Negotiating tactics	97
Chapter 12	Raising funds	102

Chapter 13	Trial by media and parliament	115
Chapter 14	The Auja River project	129
Chapter 15	Naharayim: 'The Two Rivers' project	141
Chapter 16	More hurdles	146
Chapter 17	The Mavromatis distraction	161
Chapter 18	Origins of a politician	166
Chapter 19	Striving for national unity	174
Chapter 20	The Passfield 'White Paper'	191
Chapter 21	More initiatives	198
Chapter 22	A last gasp venture into politics	205
Chapter 23	1939, threat of war and the 'White Paper'	211
Chapter 24	Struggle for unity	214
Chapter 25	Ill health catches up	225
Chapter 26	A hero's demise	228
Index		240

Figures and diagrams

Figure 1: Pinchas Rutenberg — 14
Figure 2: The site of the first power station of Tel Aviv — 16
Figure 3: Opening ceremony of the Jordan River Generator — 18
Figure 4: Father Georgi Gapon — 27
Figure 5: Georgi Gapon inspiring the workers — 28
Figure 6: Russian Revolution, 1905 — 32
Figure 7: Yavno Azef — 40
Figure 8: Maxim Gorky — 45
Figure 9: Ze'ev Jabotinsky — 50
Figure 10: Rutenberg as a young man — 54
Figure 11: Rutenberg's visa to leave Odessa — 66
Figure 12: A mature Rutenberg — 70
Figure 13: Paris Peace Conference — 71
Figure 14: Council of 'Big Four' — 74
Figure 15: Lord Nathan — 91
Figure 16: Railway carriage at site of Jaffa station — 94
Figure 17: A Half-Promised Land. Cartoon from *Punch* — 100
Figure 18: Louis Brandeis — 102
Figure 19: Chaim Weizmann — 105
Figure 20: Lord Melchett (Alfred Mond) — 107
Figure 21: Lord Northcliffe — 116
Figure 22: Sir Joynson-Hicks M.P. — 122

Figure 23: Winston Churchill	125
Figure 24: Abraham Rutenberg	132
Figure 25: Reading Power Station as it is today	138
Figure 26: Naharayim, the Two Rivers Power Plant	154
Figure 27: Naharayim	155
Figure 28: Naharayim Power Plant destroyed by Jordan	156
Figure 29: Solar panels at the site of the Naharayim reservoir	156
Figure 30: Colonel Frederick Kische	167
Figure 31: Judah Magnes	175
Figure 32: Lord Passfield (Sidney Webb)'	184
Figure 33: Palestine Airways aeroplane	198
Figure 34: Sir Robert Bruce-Lockhart	221
Figure 35: Berl Katznelson	226
Figure 36: Rutenberg Institute in Haifa	236
Diagram 1: Site of Rutenberg's proposed power plant	78
Diagram 2: Disputed borders of Palestine, 1920s	82
Diagram 3: Map of railways of Palestine, circa 1920s	93
Diagram 4: Rutenberg's dams and canals at Naharayim	150
Diagram 5: Simplified diagram of Naharayim	151
Diagram 6: Partition Plan, Peel Report	208

Acknowledgements

I first came across Pinchas Rutenberg while I was researching my previous book on the early history of Israel[1] and, recognising his unique contributions to Mandatory Palestine, I was convinced that he deserved a story of his own. This was to be my first effort in writing a biography but I was hampered by the lack of any literature about him in the English language. Only two books existed, one in Hebrew[2] and the other in Russian[3]. It was inevitable that I would need help in translation and for that I turned to Emma Phillips who valiantly ploughed through the Hebrew biography for me. Sadly, much of that publication was not entirely relevant for my purposes, and I had to search rather more widely for information, scarce though this was. Rutenberg also wrote in Yiddish and here I had to rely on the expertise of Izzy Posner who bravely translated one of Rutenberg's polemics to American Jewry.

I received ideas about my presentation from many long-suffering individuals who selflessly spent time reading it. Not surprisingly, the format of the book has changed as it has evolved over the last couple of years. I originally conceived it as a novel based on Rutenberg's life but I was made aware that this may not be the best way of presenting a larger than life individual. It may be more believable if a life so full of action and incident was presented as a more factual account and I changed my view about the writing. In acknowledging the help given to me it may seem to some of those who have commented that this book is now unrecognisable compared with the one they originally saw. I hope they will forgive me but I feel that the book has been remarkably improved by the help of David Turner, Mark Regev, Victor Hoffbrand, Amina Harris, Ruth Deech, Simon MacDonald, Emanuel Grodzinsky, Andrew Roberts and Malcolm Rowland. They might not recognise it but I hope they feel that it is all the better for their help. I am grateful to Emmanuel Grodzinsky for the photograph at Figure 29 and for his support.

I am indebted to Sophia and Marcel Kral of Smallfish Designs for their invaluable help in preparing this manuscript.

Leslie Turnberg, January, 2023

---

[1] *Mandate, The Palestine Crucible, 1919-1939*. By Leslie Turnberg. Published by Vallentine Mitchell, London, 1921.

[2] *Pinhas Rutenberg:1879-1942, Life and Times*. By Eli Shaltiel. Published by Am Oved, Tel Aviv, 1990

[3] *Pinkhas Rutenberg: Ot Terrorista k sionistu*. By Vladimir Khazan. Published by Mosty Kul'tury-Gersharim. Moscow. 2008

Preface

Jewish literature is replete with biographies of great men and women who have contributed much to the history of the Holy Land. Many of these significant figures, Herzl, Weizmann, Ben Gurion, Begin, Golda Meyer and others have several biographies to their name. Others have hardly been neglected but one man seems to have been largely ignored despite his enormous contributions to developments in Mandatory Palestine. Perhaps it was because of his shady history as a Russian revolutionary and a possible assassin; or because he was such an awkward customer who, with his aggressive character, provoked strong reactions against him. Or perhaps because he abhorred publicity and made it a condition in his will that there should be no memorials to his achievements, remarkable though they were. Pinchas Rutenberg was the man who created the circumstances that allowed the development of agriculture and industry in a land with few natural resources. He persuaded the British Authorities to give him the concession to introduce hydro-electricity for the whole of Palestine. Without it, and the diesel powered electrical generators he set up, it is likely that the development of a future Jewish State would have been delayed or even been prevented. He went on to start up the commercial Palestine Airways, forerunner of El Al and, in his position as leader of the Jews of Palestine (the Yishuv), he led efforts to make peace with the Arabs.

Whatever the reason for the lack of information about a remarkable man, there has been only one book in Hebrew, another in Russian, and none about him in English literature. He is largely unknown in the West and barely recognised in Israel.

I became convinced that he deserved a much greater profile. I have only quoted recorded speech where it has been possible to authenticate it. My hope is that I might make this story of a neglected but incredible man more accessible to a wider public.

Introduction

The High Commissioner was not immediately reassured by what he knew of the man facing him. Sitting squarely in front of him, Pinchas Rutenberg's large, forbidding presence seemed to dominate the room. Sir Herbert Samuel was not a man to be easily intimidated but the glare with which Rutenberg fixed him, heightened by the afternoon sun reflected in his glasses, certainly made an impression. So, in Jerusalem, in 1920, when Rutenberg lent forward and presented Samuel with an offer, he listened warily. Rutenberg's reputation had followed him from Russia and the whiff of Lucifer still clung to him. Samuel knew that he had been a revolutionary and a fugitive, but was it also true that he had been an assassin and, as some had suggested, a Bolshevik?

Rutenberg spoke through clenched teeth as if he meant business when he presented his plans to electrify the whole of Palestine. He needed Samuel's support so that he could install his hydro-electricity generators on the Jordan River. Only in this way could he secure the future development of the land. Or so he tried to convince Samuel.

Samuel had only recently arrived to set up the Civil Administration of Palestine and, while wanting to make his mark, this offer might have seemed a little premature in the eyes of an English aristocratic gentleman. Of course, his assumed air was a façade. He had already demonstrated a keen interest in the possibility of industrial investment in Mandatory Palestine and knew that electrification would be essential. But, in 1920, he had only just assumed office as High Commissioner and had to give the impression of detachment and even-handedness. His appointment had come under fire when it was announced, and critics wondered how it might be possible for a Jew and a Zionist to remain unbiased in his dealings with the Arabs and Jews. He had to tread carefully and he revealed nothing as he concealed his enthusiasm for Rutenberg's plan.

The High Commissioner was nothing if not the supreme diplomat. He sought the opinion of Ronald Storrs, his Governor in Jerusalem, but Storrs prefered to wait until much later before offering a view.

The formalities had to be gone through before expressing support for what seemed to some like a wild idea. Although he became an early advocate for Rutenberg's scheme, Samuel well knew that the proposition was at the least precarious and certainly premature.

He was well aware that Rutenberg had yet to gain the British Government's approval for the concession he needed. Samuel was interested but not entirely optimistic. He failed to reckon with a man who was determination personified.

Pinchas Rutenberg always knew that he would achieve great things and when the opportunity arose, he grasped it with a grip of steel. It was the challenge given to him of a virgin territory, a new land, where he could make his dreams come true – the electrification of Palestine. The route to this end was full of hazards and hurdles but he was built of a single-mindedness that allowed no deviation from his purpose.

Photographs of him reveal a man frowning directly at the viewer behind round, thin-rimmed glasses (*Fig. 1*).

A broad square face topped by a thatch of dark, wavy, swept-back hair, while his short neck sits on thick-set shoulders. The whole impression is of a glowering, forbidding presence, someone you would not want to cross. A combination of 'a steam-roller and a whirl-wind' is how Lt. Colonel Frederick Kisch, Head of the Palestine Executive Committee, described him. Ronald Storrs wrote that he had a head as strong as granite and an utterance low and menacing through clenched teeth. High Commissioner, Sir John Chancellor, wrote later that he was 'an aggressive, eruptive mountain of a man who was always predicting disaster'. His friend, Louis Lipsky, said he was 'a solid mass of rebellion, with absolute convictions'. He described his behaviour as 'in intimate circles he would dilate in the commanding tones of a sergeant-major on wide-ranging plans and speak of world-encircling strategy in which his listeners were invited to help turn the world upside down'. He was someone apt to treat a difference of opinion as a personal insult; a faithful friend but a particularly disagreeable enemy. But there were many surprisingly close friends who admired, respected and even loved him. Moshe Smilansky, the farmer, prolific author and advocate for Arab-Jewish co-existence, was an admirer who wrote of him that he was full of contradictions and wrapped in secrecy and magic. He

Figure 1: Pinchas Rutenberg

went on to point out that he had a weakness for giving orders but because he, Smilansky, loved him, he always carried out those orders. There were other surprises too. His fondness for speaking Yiddish brought him into a firm friendship in New York with the Yiddish poet and scholar, Solomon Blumgarten (known as Yehoash), who thought him a 'superman'. And for a man who had lost all interest in religion he showed considerable respect for Rav Avraham Kook, Chief Rabbi of Palestine. In honour of the Rabbi, Rutenberg put his energies into re-building a Talmudic college, Yeshivat Kerem b'Yavneh, that had long been the Rabbi's dream.

Although Rutenberg certainly had had a somewhat unsavoury career before he arrived in Palestine, he was the man who, in electrifying the country, set the foundations for its industrial and agricultural development. And they were far from the only significant contributions he made to the evolution of the country.

CHAPTER 1

The lights go on in Allenby Street

Fly into Israel at night and you will be greeted by the sight of the lights of Tel Aviv glowing below you like a great twinkling carpet.

The sight maybe exciting but by now is accepted as unexceptional by a sophisticated flying public.

But it was Pinchas Rutenberg just over a hundred years ago who made it happen. An outburst of joy greeted him when he pressed the button that switched on the lights in Tel Aviv. After three years of painful negotiation with a vacillating government, Rutenberg had managed, by 10th of June 1923, to

Figure 2: Here the first power station of Tel Aviv (and Land of Israel) was situated, established by Pinchas Rutenberg in 1923

make electricity flow in Palestine. He had done so by a mixture of thorough planning, audacity and sheer Machiavellian behaviour. His diesel power plant in HaHashmal Street (Hashmal is 'Electric' in Hebrew) was a huge success and he was delighted that he had overcome considerable opposition to reach this point (*Fig. 2*).

It was in Allenby Street where the lights were lit to an ecstatic crowd. The name was symbolic. Allenby was the man who had liberated Jerusalem in 1917 and now, here was Rutenberg, opening a door to the future. Nothing stopped the cheering crowds as the lights came on. He had wanted celebrations to be muted. He did not want to stir up difficulties with the Arab population or with the Government in London, but that failed to stop the crowd carrying him to his car in joyful procession. The following day a fleet of flower-decked bicycles accompanied him as he drove through Tel Aviv. It was a great success, and the symbolism of this achievement was significant even though it had been achieved by a mixture of sleight of hand and sheer audacity (*Chapter 14*).

But he had not yet obtained the final concession for his major hydro-electric scheme on the Jordan River. Here in Tel Aviv he was making do with an interim, supposedly temporary, system of diesel-powered generation.

It was to be another nine years before electricity began to flow from his Jordan River plant and meanwhile, he had built two more diesel-powered plants and a gas and steam-generated system in North Tel Aviv. They were just as successful as the first and began to produce profits well before his hydro-electric plant got off the ground.

He had to overcome huge hurdles before electricity flowed from the Jordan River and it was only on the 9th of June 1932 that success was finally achieved here, at his major venture (*Chapter 15*).

The opening ceremony in Jaffa had not been received by much official recognition but now, here at the Jordan, there was much more pomp and ceremony. It was held in the presence of High Commissioner Sir Arthur Grenfell Wauchope (the fifth High Commissioner that Rutenberg had seen come and go since Herbert Samuel), together with the Emir Abdullah of Jordan, Colonel Cox, British Governor of the Emirate of Jordan and many other dignitaries (*Fig. 3*).

The Times, on June 10th, 1932, under the heading 'Hydro-Electric Power in Palestine. Jordan Station Opened.' was laudatory. Rutenberg was described as 'an extremely talented engineer' with unbounded energy and a great talent for

Figure 3: Opening ceremony of the Jordan River Hydro-electricity Generator. Pinchas Rutenberg with Lady and Lord Reading to his left

organisation. He was responsible for delivering the supply of electricity that Palestine desperately needed for its agricultural and industrial development. And he was able to see his plans through to success because of his matching capacity for business and entrepreneurship. He had not only masterminded the plans for the electrification schemes, both hydro and diesel powered, he had convinced a sceptical, and often hostile, British Parliament to grant him the concession to do so. Nor was everyone amongst the Zionists fully supportive either.

But it was not merely the electricity he supplied.

He provided employment for several thousand workmen at a time when unemployment in the country was running high. He encouraged immigration when it was beginning to lapse. And he created a huge financial influx from foreign investors when there was little else to attract outside funding.

There is a problem in trying to separate his ability to achieve great things on the ground from his characteristic bluntness, and serious capacity to get up everyone's nose. Against all his achievements we have to set the difficulties posed by these abrasive characteristics. It is entirely conceivable, of course, that he would not have been successful without them. Perhaps they were interdependent?

This is the story of a man who let nothing and no-one stand in his way. An unreasonable man whose achievements were remarkable in a remarkable era.

How did a man with a tarnished history as a revolutionary and possible assassin manage to achieve all that he did against huge opposition?

CHAPTER 2

A revolutionary is born

It was a life not lacking in hazardous drama involving key roles in the Russian revolutions of 1905 and 1917, arms smuggling, an assassination and hot pursuits as he was driven out of Russia. It was here too where his lack of respect for democratic principles was derived. These were his formative years and, if his future career in Palestine is to be understood, we should examine them more closely.

By 1879, the year when Rutenberg was born, revolutionary ideas were beginning to stir the people of the Ukraine and, amongst the Jews, thoughts of Zionism were being kindled.

Born in Romny, where his wealthy father was well aware of the antisemitism and pogroms to which the family were subject, Piotr (later re-named Pinchas) was acutely conscious of the plight of the peasants and the cause of the workers, and it was these, rather than the plight of the Jews, that consumed his teenage and later years. He lived a comfortable life within his relatively affluent family but he could hardly have been unaware of the desperate circumstances of the peasants in the outlying villages. Despite his early orthodox Jewish education he soon lost all feeling for religion and his thoughts were overtaken by a belief in an international socialism that, he was convinced, would incorporate the needs of the Jews. For now, he was a revolutionary in thrall to the overthrow of the Tsar.

By the age of 13 he had already developed some of the characteristics of an autocratic leader who was able to take command of his brothers and sister. His appetite for leadership led him to an intolerance of lesser mortals who were not always appreciative. Despite developing a life-long aptitude to rub people up the wrong way he was already being recognised as someone who was a leader of men. He seemed to know what needed to be done and where he was going; and others followed.

Although Yiddish was his first language and remained the one with which he was most comfortable, he learnt Russian at his Gymnasium and later could speak English and French without difficulty.

His intelligence shone through, he led in his school and he obtained one of the very few places allowed for Jews at the Imperial St. Petersburg Institute of Technology from where he graduated at the top of his class.

These were stormy years of unrest in Russia as Piotr dived headlong into the revolutionary ideas flowing through the student body of 1895. The rooms he shared with five other students left him sleeping on the floor much of the time but the cold, damp walls could not cool the heat of their debates. His eyes flashed in the enthusiastic certainties of youth as he took on the righteous self-image of a champion of the peasants. Bearded and unkempt, donned in the uniform of a revolutionary, he peered through his wire-framed spectacles at his colleagues. Like him they were of a privileged background that left them riddled by a guilt that drove them on ever more fanatically. They were absolutely certain about their responsibility for righting the wrongs they saw about them. By now, any feeling for religion he may have had had gone, to be replaced by a sense of injustice at the oppression of the peasants and workers inflicted by the Tsar. It was to be some years before he accepted the idea that the Jews, subjected to pogroms and persecution, were a special case and needed a land of their own.

In his first year at the Institute, Piotr was taken up with the romantic, populist vision of peasant village life, a harmonious society where each individual was an equal. He did not quite grasp that the peasants were not only constantly at each other's throats, they were deeply suspicious of educated students intent on improving their lot. He believed that he knew best what the proletariat needed and that there was no need to consult such an ignorant and uneducated group of people. It was this dictatorial attitude that he later took with him to Palestine where he maintained his belief that, like Russian peasants, the Jews of Palestine were to be led regardless of their own opinions. The peasants would do whatever they were told and would follow a lead into the glorious future that would be provided for them. But not yet.

It would take some time before the reality of brutish Russian village life would open his eyes and populism would make way in his mind for the Marxism that was sweeping through Russia in the 1890s. It was now the turn of the workers rather than the peasants that grabbed his attention. Marxist ideas were being explored across the student body and he was transfixed.

Convinced that he must be fully engaged, he put all his energies into spreading the revolutionary message about the new Tsar, Nicholas II, who was no improvement on the terrifying Alexander. He exhorted his colleagues to look around at the grinding poverty of the proletariat and the oppression of the workers. No help could be expected from this reviled Tsar. He was not deterred from his revolutionary zeal by the virulent anti-Semitism and the wave of pogroms being unleashed. The Jews could wait.

Revolution was the answer and only then, would the equality in a new society make the problems of the workers, and coincidentally the Jews, disappear. He soon fell out with the Marxists and then with the Bundists.

He had no time for the latter with their, to him, crazy ideas about a separate Jewish cultural autonomy within Russia. Only with a revolution that brought international socialism could relief of the oppression of the masses be achieved. Ignoring the waves of pogroms, he pressed on with his Socialist Revolutionary messages. He resisted the idea that he might be labelled as belonging to any specific grouping. He was never a convinced Marxist and did not take on the mantle of Bolshevism later. He was most concerned with righting wrongs by social activism and had his own brand of revolutionary socialism, picking up ideas from the myriad of revolutionary groups vying for attention.

Then in 1896 the obscenity of Nicholas's coronation celebrations inspired him to greater action. Almost 2,000 peasants were killed or maimed in the crush to gain the Tsar's free gifts of beer and sausages. There was plenty of room into which Rutenberg's resentment could grow. He was inflamed and, with his words flowing and his eyes flashing, he was already an imposing figure despite his obvious youth.

His friends were quick to follow him, the natural leader of men. Of the many revolutionary groups vying with each other in the aggressiveness of their credos, Rutenberg decided to join the Socialist Revolutionary Party. As a man of action, he had a life-long antipathy to politics and politicians and preferred the wing of the party concerned with 'action' to the political wing. So, it was only natural that he joined the so-called 'Fighting Organisation', the terrorist wing, in which Yevno Azef, about whom we will hear more later, was a leading figure. Piotr's activities were far from hidden. The deadly serious business of avoiding the prying eyes of the secret police, the Okhrana, kept him on his toes. They had good reason to suspect him of arms smuggling and it was not long before he was hauled before the Principal of the Institute. Out he must go as he was told that there was no room for his revolutionary nonsense in the Imperial Institute where obedience and respect for the Tsar were the absolute rule.

Head down but hardly bowed, Piotr was expelled and found himself in Moscow where he had a year to cool his heels. Here, away from the capital, he knew full well that the Okhrana were everywhere. He was apprehensive as he looked over his shoulder for friends he could trust and was immediately attracted when the oily Yevno Azef reached out to him with instructions. With his forceful stare, Azef described how he could work his way through the underground without being discovered.

An ugly, thick-set man with a strange fascination for women, Azef was already an accomplished revolutionary operator with a ruthless streak. His reputation as an assassin would soon spread as he became a hero amongst the revolutionaries. It was some years before Piotr learnt that this mentor was one of the most renowned and reviled double agents, in league with the secret police.

But who better to tutor Rutenberg in the art of smuggling arms?

Explosives were the weapons of choice and it was simple to acquire them through Finland. They were easy to transport and hide and Piotr was delighted to be learning the trade of undercover work.

Soon, however, all this clandestine activity was beginning to tell on him and he was relieved when he was allowed to return to the Technology Institute at the end of the year. And it suited his Party to have one of their men back in the Institute.

CHAPTER 3

1905, Revolution

He knew he had done well in his final examinations and when he graduated top of his class, he was pleased but not surprised. The huge Putilov iron works in St Petersburg beckoned and he was happy to be offered a job as an engineer. An industrial giant employing over 12,000 workers, the Putilov overwhelmed Piotr at first by its vastness and the deafening clatter of machines. Manufacture of shipping, tractors and, most importantly, arms and ammunition gave him dangerous but unrivalled opportunities for clandestine activity. But it was the conditions of the workers that struck him most and that re-ignited his sense of purpose. He realised that the oppression and suffering he had heard about was far from exaggerated. Long hours of drudgery and poor pay together with the threat of being thrown out of a job at the least misdemeanour was the norm. He wondered how a man could hold up his head when he was so deprived of the means of a humane existence. To be dismissed from your job for spending too much time in the lavatory or failing to reach production targets was an impossible burden. It was little wonder that there were so many strikes or that they were so ineffective when all the power lay in the hands of the owners.

He began to think that a work force of the size employed at Putilov was there waiting for someone to mobilise. Its potential for concerted action was there to be taken. And as a major manufacturer of armaments, it was ripe for secretive expropriation by his Socialist Revolutionary Party. Soon he achieved promotion in the factory and it was recognised that his engineering skills gave him credibility in the Party and amongst the men. The workers were beginning to see him as someone on their side and to turn to him to lead. He was now more convinced than ever that the overthrow of the Romanovs was vital if the workers were to gain their rights.

He seems to have had time to marry. He met and fell in love with the pretty Olga Homenko. The fact that she was a devout Christian did not deter him as by then he had lost all interest in religious observance. They had four children together, Anatol, Eugene, Lara and Rochelle. Some years later, when Piotr (by then re-named Pinchas) left Russia for Palestine, he worked hard to extricate his family. He managed to get them to Paris where he visited them, but Olga was not the least interested in a Jewish homeland in Palestine or in Rutenberg's burgeoning obsession with hydro-electricity. The marriage could not last and she and her children left for America. It is unlikely that they saw each other again and may not even have corresponded.

Figure 4: Father Georgi Gapon

Nineteen hundred and five was to be a busy year for Piotr. It started with his role with Father Gapon in leading the strike that led to the disastrous loss of life in the abortive revolution of that year. It ended with his arrest in Finland for his part in smuggling arms from England.

Father Georgi Gapon had a mystical air that made his thin, gaunt face, framed by thick hair and a long beard, seem almost saintly (*Fig. 4*). With dark, magnetic eyes, he had an inspiring way with words and had gathered a huge number of followers to the cause that he espoused for them (*Fig. 5*). Not a revolutionary, he was a man of the cloth, against violence, and suspicious of those revolutionaries led by educated intellectuals and students. But he was desperate to improve the lot of the workers. He suffered with the men working eleven and a half hours a day for pitiful pay and subject to summary dismissal.

Figure 5: Georgi Gapon inspiring the workers

Rutenberg was captivated on hearing Gapon press a large group of workers to strike yet again as conditions worsened. He was fascinated by the small, thin man as he inspired everyone with his words. This time, he told them, the strike would be much better organised than it had been until then. Rutenberg was surprised and delighted when Gapon turned to him and asked him to assist him in his work. And by then Piotr knew that he would be able to command a following at his factory.

Gapon was certainly an inspirational speaker but Rutenberg became anxious when Gapon told him that he was not a revolutionary. He was suspicious that Gapon, although motivated by the suffering of the workers, thought the best way of helping them was to engage directly with the Tsar on their behalf.

Rutenberg did not think for one moment that the Tsar or his court would pay more than lip service to such an appeal. As it turned out he was perfectly correct.

Gapon's technique was to try to influence the Tsar and his high officials directly by persuasion. He had gained the attention of senior figures in the security forces with his writings about the plight of the workers, but acting as a go-between was fraught with danger and Rutenberg recognised that here was where Gapon's misfortune would lie. Gapon even had the support of the Okhrana when he set up the 'Assembly of Russian Factory and Mill Workers of St. Petersburg', an early Trades Union of sorts. Sergeus Vasileyvitch Zubatov, the chief of the political section of the Police Department, was delighted to have someone in close contact with the workers and who could exert influence over them.

Gapon believed he could gain concessions while Zubatov simply used him to gain knowledge of the workers' plans and passed on his information to the Okhrana. For the moment Rutenberg was unaware of the dangerous liaison between Gapon and the enemy. But it left the priest open to the later accusation of the treachery that was to lead to his undoing.

His motives seemed selfless; his methods doomed, and the consequences for both Rutenberg and Gapon were profound. One was to be assassinated and the other had to flee.

Rutenberg watched with growing apprehension as unrest in the Putilov factory grew. It came to a head when four workers were dismissed for very little reason. In vain did Piotr and the leaders of the Workers Assembly argue for their reinstatement. There was an insatiable demand for a massive strike and it would have only been avoided if the owners of the factory had heeded the workers' plea.

January, 1905 and Gapon decided to act. St. Petersburg was bitterly cold as he travelled by sledge from factory to factory gaining support for strike action. He pressed the bosses and the chief of police to try to come to terms and re-instate the four workers, but by the time they agreed it was just too late. The strike scheduled for the 22nd of January was unstoppable.

And now twenty-six years old Rutenberg, already heavily involved in his revolutionary party, was primed for action and the proposed strike saw him busily spreading the message to the workers.

Gapon looked exhausted after a night of frantic negotiations as he faced Rutenberg. He showed Piotr the petition he intended to present to the Tsar. It read, 'We working men of St. Petersburg, our wives and children and our parents, helpless, aged men and women have come to you, oh Tsar, in quest of justice and protection. We have been beggared, oppressed, overburdened with excessive toil … We are not recognised as normal human beings but are dealt with as slaves who have to bear their bitter lot in silence. The awful moment has come when death is better than the prolongation of our unendurable tortures'. Rutenberg could hardly contain himself as he read, 'O Emperor, there are more than three hundred thousand of us here, yet we are all of us human beings only in appearance and outwardly, while in reality we are deemed devoid of a single human right, even that of speaking, thinking, and meeting to talk over our needs, and of taking measures to better our condition. Is life under such laws worth living?'

Gapon would not allow himself to believe that Tsar Nicholas could refuse the supplications he now put forward, if, of course, he was ever able to read them.

A huge number of striking workers and their wives and children gathered for their march on the Winter Palace. Their excitement was hardly dispelled by the grey clouds threatening another snow-storm. Here at last was action instead of mere words thought Piotr Rutenberg as he shivered and pulled his coat tightly around his thick frame.

Gapon was pressing him to help lead what he fondly thought of as a 'delegation'. But Piotr was worried. It was all very well striking while the iron was hot but should they not have some arms in case things go wrong and they were attacked by the Tsar's men? Gapon would not hear of it. He firmly believed that as men of peace the police would not dare to fire on them. A man of God and a group of unarmed citizens could not possibly be met by armed opponents. Already a canny fighter, Rutenberg felt differently. He would never place his trust in the Tsar.

Gapon made the big mistake of persisting in his belief that they would not be harmed. He ordered his men to enter a church and gather religious symbols and icons to parade in front of the crowd as they marched. And if these were not enough to protect them, he had a portrait of the Tsar raised on a staff at the fore. Rutenberg remained apprehensive and, as it turned out, with very good reason. He was a better judge of the behaviour of oppressors and when he was encouraged to address the crowds, he included information about where arms were hidden. Gapon and the workers ignored the hint.

At 10am the huge, unarmed, crowd of men, women and children marched steadily towards the Winter Palace singing a hymn to the Holy Orthodox Church. There they met the Tsar's forces. Told that the strikers were intent on seizing the Winter Palace and slaughtering the Royal Family, the troops were primed for action (*Fig. 6*). Gapon was not at the

Figure 6: Russian Revolution, 1905

front but shielded in the second line by bodyguards. No-one listened and no-one stopped as the Cossacks drove into them hacking mercilessly left and right as they rode back and forth through the crowds. Then the troops raised their rifles and began to fire. A massacre. Hundreds of men, women and children dropped wounded or bleeding to death while others fled screaming on this horrendous 'Bloody Sunday'. Two of Gapon's bodyguards were killed and he fell to the ground amongst bleeding bodies. Rutenberg grabbed him, pulling him to the side and away from the gunfire. Urging him to run they skidded through the icy snow until Rutenberg grasped some scissors and hurriedly trimmed Gapon's beard. He stripped him of his cassock and hat and covered him in the blood-stained coat and cap of a passing worker. They quickly found some safety in the house of a friend of Rutenberg. Rapidly shaving off the rest of his beard and changing him into peasant clothes, on they moved from friend to friend until they came at last to the relative safety of Maxim Gorky's house.

Gorky, an intellectual writer with a high profile, even then was a good friend of Rutenberg and we will meet him later in Italy. He gave them but a day of security. Chaos across the city saw the workers marching along multiple routes converging on the Palace, only to be halted by hails of bullets. The riots, that by now the strikes had become, continued to rage for another two days leaving at least 200 dead and 800 wounded.

Gapon and Piotr could hardly relax as the police roamed the streets. There was little they could do but escape from St. Petersburg. The fires of revolution that had then been lit in 1905 led inexorably to the Revolution of 1917.

But by 1906 Rutenberg became embroiled in an event that cast a long shadow over his future life. The assassination of Father Gapon. It was this violent act that almost blighted his efforts, fifteen years later, to gain the concession from the British Government for the electrification of Palestine.

CHAPTER 4

Assassination

As they escaped, there was no hint yet that Piotr Rutenberg was going to be involved in the murder of his colleague. They zig-zagged together on foot through snow-covered fields sheltered by helpful farmers and were eventually smuggled across a barbed-wire fence into the relative safety of Prussia. Perhaps Gapon was already finding Rutenberg difficult to deal with. He failed to mention him in the autobiography he wrote later while in exile in London. He simply wrote about 'the engineer' who helped him escape the slaughter Nowhere did he suggest that Rutenberg travelled with him in the adventure story he wove of his tortuous escape across Russia. Nor did he describe how Piotr miraculously appeared in Geneva, Paris and London to introduce him to revolutionaries. In Geneva, Lenin in exile was at home when Piotr brought Gapon to meet him as the hero of 'Bloody Sunday'.

Lenin was cautious in his reception and understood more than others that Gapon was no revolutionary. The sense of suspicion was mutual as Gapon avoided mention in his biography of any contact with Lenin. His reticence is surprising because he stayed with the anarchists, Peter Kropotkin and Rudolf Rocker while in London when he was commissioned to write his biography. There is no mention of them nor of Lenin and the leading communists he met in Geneva, or of Clemenceau and the Socialists in Paris. Perhaps an aversion to the revolutionaries led him to avoid describing these meetings but he was certainly welcomed and entertained lavishly while in Europe. Rutenberg was starting to lose faith in Gapon who began to live a rather louche life in the nightclubs of Paris and the casinos of Monte Carlo. Perhaps hardly surprising that Gapon did not mention these escapades in his biography.

Rutenberg was worried and decided to try to straighten Gapon out. Who better to help than the head of the 'Fighting Organisation' of the Socialist Revolutionary Party, Yevno Azef, now conveniently ensconced in Geneva. Azef put the fear of God, literally, into Gapon and, with his persuasive glare, helped Gapon tidy up his act. He helped pull him together by persuading him to focus on how much he was needed by the workers struggling in Russia. He must return home and to help them as only he knew how. This was a meeting that had profound consequences for Gapon in due course. But it is not only the Social Revolutionary Party that wanted him home. The secret police, the Okhrana, were pressing him too. They relied on him for their dirty work.

He agreed to return. Piotr made sure he kept to his word and by early 1906 he was back in St. Petersburg.

Meanwhile, during the time when Gapon was writing his autobiography in London, Piotr was having adventures of his own. It was Azef, again, weaving his dangerous spell in Geneva, who approached him with a mission. He appointed him as head of the Party's organisation responsible for acquiring arms and ammunition and immediately sent him off to England to meet some friendly plotters. The purpose was to buy the arms that were needed and to hire a boat to bring them back to Russia. Azef had already arranged the funding. Piotr was not to know that the money for the deal had been supplied by the Japanese military to help the Revolutionaries undermine the Tsar's regime. Such were the international politics involved in shady deals. *Plus ça change.*

That Rutenberg was by now a revolutionary is beyond doubt. Later, he was to be accused of being a terrorist. But was he simply an insurgent or freedom fighter? Whatever definition is chosen, it was difficult to escape the accusations of terrorism when he travelled to Britain to gather arms.

Sneaking his way through France and on to the Dutch port of Amsterdam, he reached the docks. A teeming mass of merchants and sailors made it easy for Piotr to bribe his way aboard a ship loaded with goods headed for England. By May he was meeting Russian socialist exiles in the East End of London and had managed to acquire a huge stash of guns, bullets and explosives.

The good ship 'John Crafton' was moored in the Thames and with his cash at the ready, Piotr ensured that the crew closed their eyes as the goods were loaded at night. Not a very 'good' ship as it turned out. Loaded to the gunnels, and listing heavily, it chugged erratically across the North Sea towards Finland. Never a good sailor, Rutenberg was feeling unwell as they approached the Finnish coast when disaster struck.

Limping towards a secluded cove, the ship became grounded on some rocks. Fearing detection, the crew panicked and hurriedly started burying some of the arms and then much to Rutenberg's dismay blew up the rest with the ship. The crew scattered like ants through the trees but Piotr was discovered by the guards and arrested. Handed over to the Tsar's police he soon found himself in jail again. He did manage to reach Azef with information about the whereabouts of the buried arms and at least some were salvaged for the cause. Kicking his heels in prison he reflected uncomfortably on the fiasco. But at least he had made his mark in the Party and with the feared Azef. He now had his credentials embellished by the period of incarceration that every revolutionary needed.

Out of jail and back in St. Petersburg by January 1906, he soon caught up with his erstwhile colleague, Father Georgi Gapon.

The long Russian winter had not yet lost its grip and a feeble sunshine had hardly broken its icy spell. Gapon turned to Rutenberg, and fixed him with his dark, deep-set eyes. Piotr was already aware that Gapon was averse to revolution and inclined to try persuasive argument with the authorities. Piotr knew this approach to be without any prospect of success but there was no mistaking Gapon's new message. Would Rutenberg join him and work more closely with the Tsar and his officials, albeit on behalf of the workers? Rutenberg was aghast that his friend was pressing him to work with the forces of evil and the conversation must have shaken him.

Although he knew that Gapon had had contacts with the secret police, Rutenberg was faced with the full extent of those contacts and the realisation of what was now being suggested.

Slowly Gapon edged towards admitting that he had been in league with the police for some time.

It was Pyotr Rachkovsky, one of the Heads of the Okhrana, and Gapon's puppet master, who suggested that they should try to bring Rutenberg over to their side with a huge bribe of 25,000 Roubles.

Rutenberg was now outraged and when Gapon suggested that it might be a good time for Piotr to join him he could barely control himself. All those friends and colleagues recently slaughtered by those with whom he was now being asked to work was too much to bear. Burdened with this knowledge he went away confused and anxious about what he should do. After all, Gapon had been his friend and mentor. But should such a traitor be allowed to survive? He was conflicted and vacillated but despite his hesitation Gapon certainly finished up dead. But the circumstances surrounding his assassination are shrouded in intrigue as the blame was shifted from one to the other.

Rutenberg decided that he must expose Gapon to the leaders of his Party.

Shifty silence met his announcement that there was a traitor who needed to be dealt with. His erstwhile colleagues were keen to avoid having to do away with such a prominent and important leader of the workers. But it was inevitable that, when Yavno Azef heard of it, Gapon's head had to fall. Azef had no compunction. Or mercy. Rutenberg knew full well that Azef had earned his spurs as the mastermind in the assassination of Vyacheslav Plehve, Minister of the Interior, and Grand Duke Sergei Alexandrovich, the Tsar's uncle. He now had considerable prestige and was head of the combat division (terrorist section) of the Party (*Fig. 7*). Piotr was not going to say 'no' when Azef passed sentence.

But what no-one knew, and certainly not Rutenberg, was that Azef was also the highest paid police informant of the time and a treacherous double agent responsible for revealing deadly information about revolutionaries to the Okhrana.

Azef now worried whether Gapon had got wind of his treachery when he sheltered him in Geneva the previous year. Perhaps Gapon would be tempted to expose him? He could not risk it and that, in the end, was the deciding factor in Gapon's fate.

But it was Rutenberg who turned out to be the fall guy responsible.

Using an assumed name, he rented a dacha in a small town, Ozraki, north of St. Petersburg, and lured Gapon out there for more discussions. What transpired there is unclear, but the end result was that Gapon finished up hung by his neck.

Figure 7: Yavno Azef

Rutenberg had arranged for three militants to sit silently in an adjoining room to listen to Gapon's admission and when they burst into the room to impose justice he later described how he left them get on with their work. But that version of events did not seem to satisfy his comrades and when Gapon's decomposing body was discovered a month later hanging from a hook in the cottage, his erstwhile comrades denied all knowledge of it.

Was it Rutenberg's three comrades who killed Gapon or did Rutenberg alone murder him?

He was certainly incensed enough and the slender Gapon would have been no match for the powerfully built Rutenberg. He could easily have knocked Gapon unconscious and slung his body by the neck on a rope. He could then have left the cottage with its gruesome contents, quietly locking the door behind him. Rutenberg always denied that particular story and placed the blame on the three assassins. It mattered little to his accusers that one of them, clearly an eye-witness, gave an account later that matched Rutenberg's own recollections.

Filled with remorse at the murder of his friend he told Boris Savinkov, Azef's number two, how saddened he was that it had to end this way. He believed that Gapon was a good man at heart. He meant well and all his feelings were for the workers. A terrible pity that he just chose the wrong way to work so closely with the enemy. A sad end for such a man, even though justice had been done.

That he was implicated as an accessory seemed undeniable and it mattered little to him that several years later he was cleared by his Party of a direct role in the murder. Azef, of course, denied all knowledge of the affair and placed all the blame on Rutenberg. The accusation of a role in assassination came back to haunt Rutenberg a few years later when he was pressing the British Government for the hydro-electric concession, but for now he was expelled from his Party because of it and, fleeing from the secret police, finished up in Italy.

CHAPTER 5

Escape to Italy

Thrown out of Russia in 1907 and pursued by the secret police, he found himself in Italy. Implicated in a nasty assassination he was also being chased by his own Socialist Revolutionary Party. He had hoped that the fuss of Father Gapon's murder would soon die down and it was with some relief that, although something of a shock and widely reported, the assassination was not regarded as entirely unusual. But he was never to escape the taint of murder and even the prospect of some respite in Italy only gave him temporary relief. He left Russia saddened and disillusioned about his future. He would have been even more distressed if he had known that it would be ten long years before he could return to his homeland.

It was during this time that he slowly became convinced that Palestine should be a Jewish homeland, and coincidentally, where he could fulfil the engineering ideas that were beginning to occupy his mind. These were the twin drivers to his development that matured during his Italian years.

Making friends with expat Russians and Italian socialists he surprised himself by becoming involved with the Zionists even though he would never like the idea that he might be considered a Zionist himself. Too nationalistic for his internationalist visions.

As he slowly came to accept the implications of being a Jew, and wrestling with his conscience, he changed his name from Piotr to Pinchas. Trotsky, born the same year as Piotr and similarly born into a wealthy Jewish family, took rather longer than Piotr to allow his revolutionary zeal to mature. Until he was 23, Trotsky was Leiba Bronstein. But Rutenberg, unlike many revolutionaries, retained his surname.

Piotr was now Pinchas; much more Jewish and it signalled the beginning of his conversion.

The idea of Jewish nationhood and a land in which it might be fostered was gaining momentum in Italy as elsewhere and Pinchas faced an internal conflict. Recognising at last that he was Jewish, he began to accept the reality of the pogroms and the persecution suffered by his mother and father.

The Italy of 1907 was in political turmoil. It had been some 36 years since its unification had been completed and a strong sense of nationalism continued to run through society. Mixing with vocal left-wing Italians, Rutenberg was swept up in the wider mood and began to think that, just as pride in nationhood was so attractive to Italian socialists, perhaps Jewish nationhood should also be given a chance.

The Italian Jewish defence organization, Pro-Causa Ebraica, was making its presence felt and Rutenberg could hardly have ignored it. Attending their meetings, he was slowly persuaded that there was indeed no other solution for the problems of the Jews than a separate distinct Nation in their own land. He had slowly come home to Herzl's vision and he began to put all his considerable energy into, what was for him, a new cause.

He was starting to believe that, by 1914, the threatened war in Europe might see Britain and France the victors against not only Germany but also the Ottomans. If the latter would loosen their grip on Palestine perhaps a victorious Britain would look kindly on a Jewish home in that part of the Middle East. The idea was being muted widely amongst the Zionists and Rutenberg latched onto it with alacrity.

Hitherto he was convinced that the Jews of the Pale should be patient and wait for the revolution. But now, in Italy, he was at last beginning to have doubts. He started to think that his socialist ideology may not be entirely appropriate when he could see that the workers and peasants were just as anti-Semitic as the Tsar.

He was torn by the rowdy debates about Marxism amongst the large number of expat Russian revolutionaries who congregated in Maxim Gorky's apartment (*Fig. 8*). Recently released from the Peter and Paul Prison in St Petersburg, Gorky was now in exile and on his way to Capri. But for the moment he was holding court in Milan.

Figure 8: Maxim Gorky

He launched into a Marxist polemic. Pinchas as ever was in awe of his friend's facility with words and listened spellbound. Gorky focussed on the continuing humiliation and brutalisation of the people, crying out to be rescued from an unimaginable torment of poverty and deprivation. He was transfixed as Gorky inspired his listeners, sitting around in comfort and freedom, not to spurn their comrades in their time of need. The Tsar and the aristocracy had to be overthrown and revolution was the only way.

By then Pinchas was not convinced that Lenin and Trotsky's brand of Bolshevism would provide the answers and the vexing question of the Jewish problem continued to gnaw away at his soul. And Gorky too, who remained a strong friend to Rutenberg, was later to lose his love-affair with Bolshevism. He came to regard Lenin as a self-seeking dictator and a traitor to the cause.

Soon a strange young man worked his way into Rutenberg's circle. As a journalist for the socialist newspaper, *Avanti!*, the 25 year old Benito Mussolini was a committed socialist, and already his leadership qualities were becoming obvious. Pinchas found his dictatorial tendencies qualities to which he could resonate. With his lips pursed, and his jaw jutting forward like the brow of a ship, Mussolini expanded on the virtues of 'syndication', his brand of socialism, to a circle of Italians to which Pinchas now turned. At the time it mattered little that Mussolini bore his brand of socialism somewhat superficially, or that by 1912 it was to be subsumed into the fascism that characterised his scramble for the dictatorship at the top of the Government. The Rutenberg connection to Mussolini was later used by the British Government as a surreptitious backchannel.

It was here, amongst the Italian socialists, that Rutenberg began to see an answer for the plight of the Jews. He put his full weight behind the idea that, in 1914, as war was about to begin, the Jews should form an armed force to fight along-side the Allies army. Such a force could help release Palestine from the Ottomans and pave the way for a Jewish homeland.

He began to try to convince his vacillating Italian socialist friends that in a war, Britain and its allies would be the victors. He was firmly of the view that Italy should take sides with Britain and France who would undoubtedly win the war. The Italians should hardly let the opportunity go by. He repeatedly warned anyone who would listen that if they joined the Germans, they would inevitably lose. Despite wide-spread strikes against the Government and much to Rutenberg's irritation, the Italian government decided to join the Triple Alliance against Britain and France. Rutenberg thought that that was a dangerous decision for Italy and now made it his determined objective to help in the setting up of a Jewish brigade to fight on the Allies side.

Despite his efforts being undermined by the waxing and waning of 'neutrality' amongst his Italian supporters, by 1914, with his characteristic unbound energy he was rushing across Europe to try to gain support for the Jewish fighting force.

Now, having lost support in Italy, he was determined as ever and was off to try his luck with the British Government.

He believed his leadership qualities were in demand and his self-confidence was hardly dented in London when he met Chaim Weizmann. Weizmann did not fully share Rutenberg's opinion of himself. Here was Weizmann, wearing the mantle of the supreme diplomat in 1914, exerting his influence on senior Government ministers to support the Zionists' cause, when the brash, incautious Rutenberg burst his way onto the scene. Weizmann was still three years away from his success with the Balfour Declaration and he did not want anyone or anything to upset his delicate negotiations. Fearing that if he did not control Rutenberg he would not only upset his sensitive discussions with Balfour and Churchill, he might upset the Jews of Germany and throw them into the hands of Britain's future enemy.

Weizmann feared that he would blunder in and destroy everything he was trying to do.

Of course, that type of resistance would never stand in Pinchas's way. He may not even have noticed the rather cool reception he was given by the Zionists. On he marched pressing his case with officials and ministers wherever he could, even grabbing the ear of Ramsay MacDonald, leader of the Labour Party, for half an hour. How he managed to engage with senior politicians, as a man recently engaged in revolutionary activities, is a mystery. His strong socialist background clearly helped with the Labour Party but his capacity to engage with officials knew few bounds.

His message was simple. Allow him to recruit a brigade of soldiers from amongst Britain's Jewish citizens to fight with them against the coming German onslaught. They could be most helpful to Britain if they were to be allowed to help guard Britain's Middle Eastern front against the Turks in Palestine.

It mattered little to Rutenberg that Turkey had not yet entered the war and that their intentions were, as yet, unclear. Hardly a surprise then that MacDonald would have nothing to do with his ideas and when Weizmann disowned Rutenberg's claim for Government attention, that was the end of it. At least for the time being. Pinchas returned to Italy empty handed but it would have been quite out of character for him to accept defeat so easily. He never did let go of his scheme for a Jewish brigade to fight on Britain's side. He was far from alone with the idea as we will see.

In the next chapter we will pursue his efforts in America to gain support for the aims of the Jews, but he had not simply used his time in Italy solely in gaining his new found Jewish nationalism. Importantly Italy was where he garnered his expertise in hydro-electricity that was to be the basis of his major contribution to the Jewish state he envisaged.

It was now that, as an engineer, he became fascinated by the new ways in which the power of water could be harnessed to create electricity. It had only been twenty years since the first turbines, driven by water, had generated electricity and now hydro-electric power plants were being installed in America and Europe. He mused that here was the way forward. Now to America.

CHAPTER 6

In America

Rutenberg met Vladimir Jabotinsky (now re-named Ze'ev Jabotinsky) in Italy in 1915. They made a striking pair: thickset Rutenberg with his domineering gaze and the small, slender Jabotinsky, whose intelligent eyes glinted amusedly behind thin spectacles (*Fig. 9*). His appearance was deceptive. An intellectual with a steely will, Jabotinsky would go on, in the 1920s, to encourage a large number of followers to his right-wing Betar group in Poland. He was more than a match for Rutenberg.

Figure 9: Ze'ev Jabotinsky

He was scouring Europe for Jewish recruits to fight against the Central Axis powers and had come down to Brindisi from Paris to meet Rutenberg to gain his support.

Rutenberg, by now convinced of the Jewish case, was a ready recruit.

Jabotinsky needed funds for the cause and wanted to ensure that Rutenberg and he did not step on each other's toes. They agreed a division of responsibility. Rutenberg should take America and he would concentrate on Europe. Looking straight into his eyes, Jabotinsky was irresistible to a Rutenberg poised for action.

Jabotinsky would work with Joseph Trumpledor to try to convince the British Army to allow them to train Jews to fight with them against the Turks. Trumpledor became the most decorated Jewish soldier in the Russia army after his involvement in the war against the Japanese. He lost an arm in that action and was already regarded as a Russian hero by the time he reached Palestine in 1912. He was taken on by the British Army to lead a Legion of Jewish volunteers to fight with the British. He led what became known as the 'Zion Mule Corps' that saw action in Gallipoli. He later became a Jewish national hero when he lost his life in his efforts to defend Tel Hai in the north against Arab invasion. Jabotinsky, Trumpledor and Rutenberg formed a formidable trio of men intent on defending the Jews of Palestine by armed means. They set about agreeing their respective roles.

Jabotinsky would go to London to gather volunteers amongst the Jews of the East End of London. Rutenberg's job would be to raise desperately needed funds by convincing wealthy American Jewry to take more interest in Zionism.

As Jabotinsky and Rutenberg basked in the sun in 1915 they hatched their plans and by the time Rutenberg returned to Milan he was ready for action. But America was attractive for more than one reason. He could try to raise funds there but he was also aware that by the turn of the century water-power had become increasingly harnessed to generate electricity across America.

Here then would be his opportunity to learn more lessons.

It was a challenge he would not resist although his hydro-electric plans were to remain quietly germinating until 1919 when he revealed his grand idea at the Paris Peace Conference.

But for now he was arriving in New York on a bright spring day in May 1915, and was immediately faced with a Jewish population in some disarray in a country keen to remain neutral in the European war.

He gained access to all the leading members of the Jewish community but soon found that they were far from uniform in their views of Zionism and the future of Jewish nationhood.

Nor did they agree on much else. It is little wonder that Jewish immigrants, having arrived in their 'teeming masses', were taking time to adjust. And the attitude towards these poor Yiddish speaking immigrants by the established, wealthy, community, largely German, was somewhat distant. Not only that, but because Zionism in Germany was still alive and well, and patriotism there ran high, it was little surprise that Pinchas faced reticence in his bid for funds to fight against Germany on Britain's side. Another reason for him to back-pedal on the idea of a Jewish Brigade. He did not take too much notice of the poorer immigrants; he was after all seeking funds from the well-off, but he could hardly have been unaware that immigrants, recently escaped from the Tsar's oppressive anti-Semitic rule, would be unlikely to offer support for a force to fight on Russia's side as Britain's ally. He had also been warned off including anything about fighting against Turkey. Supreme Court Justice Louis Brandeis in particular was anxious about upsetting the Turks if there was too much talk of taking over part of the Ottoman Empire for the Jews without their compliance. He at least knew, if Rutenberg did not, that President Wilson was a strong Turcophile and the US never did join the war against Turkey.

And he was caught in the middle between the Zionists intent on a Palestinian homeland for the Jews and others, of a more liberal view, who believed that salvation for the Jews may lie anywhere in the world. For the latter, Palestine would simply form a spiritual and cultural centre for the Jews.

His polemic, delivered to American Jewry in 1915 provides a clear indication both of his recently developed devotion to the Jewish cause and his love for, and regrets about, his mother Russia.

Reading Rutenberg's pamphlet would not leave anyone with an impression of reticence. Not much about a Jewish Brigade perhaps, but enough to make a few American ears prick up.

Written in Russian while in Italy with a title that conveys something of its stirring language – 'The National Rejuvenation of the Jewish People'– it was his call to arms. Released under the pseudonym, Pinchas Ben Ami, it had been translated into Yiddish for general (Jewish) consumption. 'Ben Ami', meaning 'son of the people', was a surprising title for a person who was nothing if not his own man.

The flowery language, written when he was 34 years old, has all the zeal and high-flown ideas of a much younger teenage revolutionary (*Fig. 10*). It was a verbose attempt to raise the pulse of disinterested onlookers as he urged Jews everywhere, but especially in America, to unite as a people with a common aim. He wanted to inspire them to look beyond their own narrow horizons at a much bigger goal.

The Paper reveals much about his own character and personal ambitions. The conflicts between his feelings for Russia and his desire to settle, once and for all, the problems of the Jews, came across clearly.

'From the depth of my soul I hate Russia's leaders for much, but mainly for their gruesome, never-before-heard-in-history, insane, as-if-boiled-from-a-heated-brain, wildly unrestrained, sick-promiscuous, Jew-torturing. But I love Russia. I am convinced that especially now, in the current war, Russia will free itself from its 'internal enemy' – the degenerate, talentless, criminal autocracy. And that together with her allies she will win against her terrible external enemy – Germany.'

Figure 10: Rutenberg as a young man

Here is a sense of his patriotism and of his use of several words where a couple would do. He makes sure his point is understood. Later he writes, 'I love Russia, my country of birth, both for the few joys and for the many big sorrows, for everything that she gave me, with which she watered my soul. I am tied to her with body and life'.

Here is his dilemma – his love-hate relationship with Russia and why he was so keen to return there when Kerensky called after the Revolution of February 1917. But the rest of his document is the strongest case possible for a Jewish State of their own in Palestine. Strain every sinew to attain it, he demands.

'Above everything we are Jews. And above all else we must protect our own Jewish interests, fulfil our own Jewish obligations. We need to step up with dignity as fit for our people. It is the whole Jewish people who have the right and the might to speak. On the American Jews lies a special, big responsibility… Time isn't waiting. The American Jews must fulfil their duty.'

After enlarging on the anti-Semitism that riddles Russian society and permeates even other, more democratic civilised countries, he goes on to call for Jews to unite in a common aim. 'Jewry has survived throughout the millennia in spite of extraordinarily unfavourable conditions.' But, 'We are the creators and carriers of invaluable world treasures – monotheism, Christianity, capitalism, international socialism – i.e. the idea of respect, brotherhood, love and cooperative help amongst people …' He repeats the words 'capitalism' and 'socialism' in the same sentence later when he makes it clear that only in a land of their own will the Jews be safe and secure. Only by two means can the 'Jewish question' be resolved; either kill them all off, or, if the Jews 'get the possibility of an independent, creative, national life in a state of their own, in their own territory, with their own science, Jewish art, industry and trade, Jewish clericalism, capitalism, socialism, class struggle, and everything, everything in which accumulated national energy could pour out in healthy, unique and intimate, national forms suited for herself. Just as with other people', that should be done. Quite a sentence, but here is more than a hint that capitalism and socialism can coexist and indeed he went on to demonstrate that point quite clearly in the development of his hydro-electric programme. It is only Palestine where this could be achieved. 'And only in the land of Israel, that with her the people's epics and the people's romance is bound, that has already attracted the creators of a significant Jewish colonisation – the beginnings of a serious Jewish culture.'

While he was anxious not to make too much of his campaign for a Jewish armed brigade to fight with the Allies he could not resist leaving a sentence or two on arms for the Jews. 'We should recognise our right to an independent national existence … and this recognition we can only get through weapons in Jewish hands; only then when we will spill our Jewish blood on that country and for that country. However small our army might be, it must be a Jewish one.'

But he had little time for those Jews he saw as simply talkers or those who were against Jewish Statehood. 'We will find our main opposers amongst out own ranks – the socialists, Bundists, Zionists, territorialists, Yiddishists, Hebraists, assimilationists, all equally intolerant, 'unhelpful', fanatical, mutually hateful, spiritually crippled from our unfortunate life, torn and unsettled.' He has special criticism for the Zionist movement and its leadership, although without mentioning Weizmann to whom he had already taken a dislike. It is not through 'lobbyists and smooth talkers' that we will fulfil our aims. 'The Zionists have awakened the consciousness of self-respect in our people; they have pointed him to the only option – the Land of Israel.' But, 'they have their overestimated belief in the power of high 'connections', lobbying, negotiations, diplomacy, means that are in no way sufficient to achieve an aim as invaluable as that which they have set themselves. … through diplomatic activity and through political activism one cannot create a state.' For a man of action, cautious diplomacy was an anathema. This was still two years before Weizmann's historic achievement in convincing the British Government to issue the Balfour Declaration. Rutenberg clearly misjudged the power of diplomacy in high places.

He went on to enlarge on his message. 'This is not about philanthropy, about love of humanity, not about establishing a 'home for oppressed and persecuted', but about solving the world-nightmare that is called the 'Jewish question. And in this everyone has equal interest, everyone must mobilise everything that is in his power – Jews and non-Jews – from all countries, all fates, all cases. It is a crime to hide oneself now, to dither and to be scared to talk loudly about our painful situation that has become impossible. Everything that depends on us, that is in our power, we are obliged to do. Right now, for our own protection, for our own salvation. We need to get rid of all our fears, all uncertainties. We have nothing to lose anyway. It can't get worse and we can win everything. No-one will stand up for us if we won't stand up for ourselves.'

And he ends by a call to arms; 'The aim should be – a Jewish state in the Land of Israel and a humane-dignified existence wherever Jews live in the diaspora … on the basis of political and national justice for all.'

Several themes emerge from this dramatic outburst.

First is the fearless energy that he went on to demonstrate in all his dealings later. He never flinched from expressing his views no matter who or what the authority he faced.

Secondly, his disdain for political Zionists busy in the international arena. A man of action himself he failed to grasp the vital roles played by Weizmann and his Zionist colleagues, especially in gaining the Balfour Declaration later.

Thirdly, he demonstrated his twin loyalties to Russia and Jewish statehood. He was always most comfortable in the company of Russians, but he knew that ultimately it was a State of Israel to which he would have to give all his love and desires. It is a clue, however, as to why he was able to return to Russia to participate in the 1917 revolutions rather than simply emigrating straight to Palestine. He may have hoped, even at that late date, that a revolution would bring freedom from persecution for the Jews in a socialist Russia of equal opportunity.

Fourthly, he left open the prospect that not all Jews would need to live in the promised land. Some would live comfortably in the diaspora where they could have 'a humane – dignified existence … on the basis of political and national justice for all'. He did not say how that nirvana might be achieved but he was not with those who believed that all Jews should settle in Palestine.

Finally, he revealed how his socialism was no barrier to the entrepreneurial form of capitalism he later evinced.

A remarkable document that was received with only modest acclaim. Nevertheless, he made his mark in America with this pamphlet that he paraded widely with whomsoever would listen and with his numerous writings and by editing the newspaper, *Yiddisher Congress*.

It was Louis Brandeis who was leading the opposition to the Zionists in his so-called Congress Party that did not see Palestine as the only country for Jews. Judah Magnes, a distinguished Rabbi in New York, on the other hand, was in the Zionist camp and Brandeis's position was an anathema to him. He guarded against diluting the message of Zionism. He resigned from his offices in America and was shortly to settle in Palestine where he became President of the Hebrew University in Jerusalem. It was there that he worked with Rutenberg on peace initiatives but soon found himself out of step in what turned out to be one of his lost causes. We will meet him later.

Weizmann, waving the banner for Zionism, was holding sway in the Zionist Organisation in London, and Rutenberg could hardly have been unaware of the battle that was raging between Brandeis and Weizmann. It certainly complicated Rutenberg's plans as we will see later when US/UK rivalry interfered with his fund-raising efforts in the 1920s. But it is

Rutenberg's attitude to these two views of where salvation for the Jews should lie that most concerns us here.

Despite his antipathy to 'politics' he could not keep out of the centre of action. Felix Frankfurter, Rabbi Stephen Wise and Louis Brandeis were the key American figures supporting investment in Palestine and they enlisted Pinchas's help in the foundation of their new organisation, The American Jewish Congress. It was raised in opposition to Weizmann's Zionist Organisation and had the much more direct aim of investing in specific infrastructure and industrial development in Palestine. For Brandeis and colleagues, immigration would then follow and it was here that they split from Weizmann and his efforts to involve Britain in the foundation of the Jewish State. Rutenberg too was suspicious of the Weizmann diplomatic approach but was wise enough to recognise that efforts to gain Britain's support could not be ignored.

He was mixing increasingly with recently immigrated Russian expats with whom he felt most at home and by now he had given up on his efforts to enlist the support of a splintered American Jewry. Losing heart, it was then that he sought refuge in hydro-electricity with the New York Municipality. He managed to gain employment there and became impressed by the hydro-electric plant developed at Niagara Falls. It had its origins in the mid 19th century but was plagued by uncompleted building of canals, bankruptcy and delays. However, by 1907 the New York Public Service Commission had set up the Hydraulic Power Company of Niagara Falls. It was successfully generating electricity although it took some time before it was able to transmit electricity any distance using Nikola Tesla's ingenious system of alternating current. It was here where Pinchas Rutenberg became transfixed by the potential of hydro-electricity and by 1917 he seemed to be making a new life for himself in America. It was then that he received the call from Alexander Kerensky.

We must now divert from his journey to Palestine as mother Russia beckoned. He could not resist. That he was dedicated to the future of the Jewish State by 1915 cannot be doubted but his plans for Palestine did not stop him speeding back to Russia when Kerensky called at the start of the revolution in 1917.

CHAPTER 7

Russia beckons, 1917

He did not hesitate to respond. This time the revolution was really taking off and Kerensky was seeking his help. At last, the Tsar was being thrown off his throne and a revolutionary party was taking over. Perhaps now a new dawn would rise.

Here was Rutenberg's dilemma. Home was still Russia and gone for the moment were thoughts of Jewish Nationhood and Palestine. His attractive dream was of a socialist, egalitarian existence in which the Jews would be an integral part and in which he could play a key part. He headed the queue of the many expat Russians clamouring to return when news of the revolution broke. For many here was the promise of a new life, free of Tsarist autocratic oppression. For him, eager to be free of the internal politicking amongst the Jews of America, it added to the pressure to hasten to return when Alexander Kerensky beckoned.

Kerensky had been a brilliant young lawyer with a silver tongue when he took on the mantle of legal defender of striking workers. At one time he found himself in jail for his pains. Of a non-violent socialist persuasion, he associated closely with the Socialist Revolutionary Party in the so-called Trudovik faction.

The February revolution had seen the Tsar deposed and the young Kerensky was a natural to become Minister of Justice in the Duma, the provisional Government. Within two months he was promoted to Minister of War and Navy and started a rapid tour of the troops around the country, encouraging them with fiery speeches. By July he was Chairman of the Provisional Guards and by September he had finally become Minister-Chairman.

Rutenberg had been a friend of the tall, thin, magnetic Kerensky some years earlier. Now Kerensky begged him to return. How could he resist when he was made Deputy Governor of Petrograd where he was put in charge of law and order. A remarkable switch for anti-authoritarian Rutenberg. Now he was caught up in Kerensky's short-lived and ill-fated regime.

Sadly, Kerensky was a much better lawyer and orator than a political leader and he failed to recognize that the mood of the people had changed, especially that of the troops. The war with Germany was being lost, there were heavy casualties and starvation and dismay had sapped the resolve of the men. Many were deserting, while life for peasants and workers was not much better.

Kerensky was losing his way in trying to stem the tide of popular opinion and in the battle against the resurgent Bolsheviks under the sway of a magnetic Leon Trotsky and Vladimir Lenin. They had become increasingly popular as they pressed for an end to the war and for a peace with the Germans. Kerensky compounded his problems by an internal dispute full of misunderstandings with his own Generals, particularly General Kornilov. He wrongly imagined that the danger of a coup from Kornilov on his right was of more danger to him than the threat of the Bolsheviks on his left. Lenin was about to launch his Bolshevik revolution and depose Kerensky's Provisional Government. Rutenberg was furious with Alexander Kerensky for not killing off Trotsky and Lenin when he had the chance. Rutenberg had form in polishing off those he opposed. The threat from Lenin and Trotsky was clear, to him at least, and doing away with them was not an entirely far-fetched idea. But it would not have been an easy solution, even if Lenin had not been in hiding elsewhere, and Kerensky in the end would not counsel it. By the 7th of November he was overthrown and it was then too late. As they huddled quietly in the basement of the Winter Palace in Petrograd, Kerensky and Rutenberg listened to the turmoil above them while revolutionary bands circled the streets. The Bolsheviks were meeting little resistance as they began to take over, and their coup was Kerensky's final undoing. When his Government fell in November 1917, he took his lieutenants, including Rutenberg, down with him. Kerensky narrowly escaped; Rutenberg, staying behind to try to defend the Government residency, did not. Kerensky's escape reads like a comic-book adventure involving a night-time run, first in a car that broke down and then in another, stolen from the American embassy and flying the US flag. Kerensky escaped first to Paris and then, when the Nazis invaded much later, in 1940, he finished up in the USA where he became one of the longest-lived revolutionaries, dying there at the age of 89. As a Mason and an atheist he was refused burial in America and finally came to rest in London at the Putney Vale Cemetery.

For Rutenberg, this was one of the most perilous moments in his life. Arrested and tried, the crowds outside were barely prevented from lynching him and his colleagues. He was whisked away to the Peter and Paul Prison where he was to spend the next few months. The reasons for his release are unclear but the end of the war with Germany and the intersession of his friend Maxim Gorky may have played a role. In any event he was free but now quite out of place under a Bolshevik regime with which he had little in common. The attempt on the life of Lenin by Fanny Kaplan on August 30th, 1918, saw the reintroduction of the death penalty and the 'Red Terror' soon followed. When 800 Socialist Revolutionaries were exterminated, Rutenberg got the message. He moved to Moscow but the longer he remained in Russia the more he would be in peril of his life and he soon secreted himself off to Odessa.

By now he had become an expert in evading capture and in slipping across borders, skills that were later to become extremely useful to him. Once in Odessa he found that the French army had taken over and that the Russian, 'White', opposition was in place. As a man with a reputation gained as a significant figure in the Socialist Revolutionary Party, he was remarkably proficient at working his way into powerful positions. He volunteered to help the French-supported

Government in exile and was soon taken on as Minister of Police. He began working closely not only with the French authorities but he also provided intelligence for British army officers. He tried to use both of those connections to his advantage later.

He was not to last long in Odessa and when the Russian 'Red' army arrived in early 1919 Rutenberg helped the French evacuation while he himself was once again on the move. Now with a Russian passport and an Exit Visa obtained by one means or another he journeyed to Constantinople, and then on to Paris via Marseille and London. By then he was an international traveller for whom borders were of little consequence (*Fig.11*).

Figure 11: Rutenberg's visa to leave Odessa

He arrived in Paris in time for the Peace Conference and it was here that his hopes and aspirations for a Russian socialist republic were subsumed into those of a Palestinian homeland for the Jews, where he could apply his expertise in hydro-electricity.

CHAPTER 8

Grand electrical plans

It had been in Italy in 1907, to where he had been banished, that he picked up his skills as a hydro-electric engineer and in America where he honed them. He was now in a position to test them out on a sceptical British and Zionist leadership.

They were not immediately fascinated by the new ways in which the power of water could be harnessed to create electricity. It was only twenty years since the first turbines, driven by water, had generated electricity and although generating plants were being installed in America and Europe, Palestine was not exactly known for its free-flowing waters. But he thought he knew better. If Palestine was ever to be successfully converted from a long-neglected backwater it would need industrialisation on a massive scale. A desert, left to ruin by the Ottomans, would have to be transformed if the Jewish dream was ever to be realised. And a supply of electricity would be absolutely essential. As Pinchas cast around for projects to engage his energies, here was the perfect opportunity. A Eureka moment for him. A virgin land where he could make a huge difference.

But he had a major problem. He knew that water had to flow at a high rate if it was to turn the powerful turbines required to generate electricity. If he was ever going to be able to obtain a sufficient flow in what was an arid desert for much of the year, he would have to come up with some ingenious ideas. He soon knew that there was only one way in which he might be able manage it. It would have to be by damming the water back at times of plenty and releasing it in times of famine. And he would need to find some rivers he could use. He began to study the building of dams and calculating water flows. By 1913 he had gained sufficient expertise to be recognised as something of an authority in the field. He knew the value of patient attention to detail and by now he was well armed and in the perfect position from which to make what became his most lasting contribution to the Holy Land and, incidentally, to the Jewish homeland.

The twin drivers of his ambitions, a successful Jewish home in Palestine underpinned by the power of hydro-electricity, had been brought together during the period of his expulsion to Italy from 1907 to 1915. Now he simply had to convince the great powers, and Great Britain in particular, in 1919 at the Peace Conference in Paris.

By 1919 he was ready to present his plans. On the face of it, Palestine would not have been the first place one would consider for producing hydro-electricity. Not much water around, with rivers likely to dry to a trickle for much of the year. There was little or no industry yet in sight to take up a supply of electricity and, by 1919, the local Arabs were already making it clear that they did not welcome any Jewish enterprises. General Allenby, who was still in command in the Military Administration, and many of his officers, were in no hurry to see the Zionists gain too much of a foothold or influence. These were just the sorts of challenges Rutenberg thrived on and he was not put off by such 'trivial' matters. Here was just the opportunity he needed to put his plans into action in a country ripe for development, and he knew he was the man to do it.

Still a young man, at the age of 40 he had already had more than a full range of experiences across Russia, Europe and America. He had participated in two revolutions and one assassination, he had met senior government figures in Italy, Great Britain and America in an effort to raise funds for the Jewish homeland idea, he had assisted in the evacuation of the French and White Russians from Odessa under threat from the Red Army, and had achieved high office in Kerensky's government and amongst the French in Odessa.

Hardly surprising then that he was greeted with joy by his fellow exiled Russian revolutionaries in Paris, who had presumed him dead, and by the Zionists who knew of his work for their cause. He tried to keep his revolutionary past and, incidentally, his involvement in assassination, under wraps but his friends made that almost impossible as they trumpeted his activities.

Figure 12: A mature Rutenberg

Paris of 1919 was the focus of the world. The post-war Peace Conference was to begin in January and, after his dramatic escape from Odessa, it was Rutenberg's opportunity to make his case on the international stage (*Fig. 12*).

He was magnetised by Paris. Everyone who was anyone was there. The American President, Woodrow Wilson, the French Premier, Georges Clemenceau and the British Prime Minister, David Lloyd George held court, sitting together to decide the future of the post-war world. How to make Germany pay, how to carve up a devastated Europe and, most significantly for the Zionists, what to do with the Ottoman's Middle East empire. New borders of old countries were decided and old borders disappeared all together. Huge numbers of supplicants milled around making their cases for a slice of the action (*Fig. 13*).

Figure 13: Paris Peace Conference

The British Government had already expressed their support for a Jewish homeland in Palestine with publication of their Balfour Declaration but would the other powers sitting in Paris accept the suggestion? Now came the anxious moment when Chaim Weizmann and Nahum Sokolov came before the committee to present the case for the Zionists. Enormous relief as they gained unanimous support. It was not, however, for a British Colonial Protectorate for the Jews but the new idea of a British Mandated Territory. This was the stricture that was imposed by Woodrow Wilson on the Europeans, in which a victor could only administer a country until it was in a position to be able to run its own affairs. Mandates were thus to be time-limited and aimed at fostering self-fulfilment of the population. In advance of Paris, Lloyd George had met the French Premier, Clemenceau, in London, and had reached an agreement that would allow France to take over Syria and Lebanon in the North and Britain to take on Mesopotamia, including Palestine, to the South. It was this that was confirmed at the Peace Conference, regardless of what the Arabs of the Middle East felt should be theirs now that the Turks had been ousted.

Weizmann and co. were overjoyed. Not so Prince Feisal with his proposal for Arab autonomy across much of the Middle East. He left Paris saddened, empty-handed and primed for revenge.

This then was the background in which Pinchas Rutenberg arrived on the scene.

He made it his business to gain support from wherever he could. Busily networking he soon gained the attention of Herbert Samuel.

Samuel had visited Palestine before he became High Commissioner and understood that, to fulfil the responsibilities of the Mandate, Britain would need to promote investment and industrialisation and the immigration of enough Jews to carry them out. He also recognised that a supply of electricity would have to be found from somewhere. So, he was well prepared for the onslaught with which Rutenberg faced him later in Jerusalem.

Rutenberg made no bones about his qualifications as the most fully trained hydro-electric engineer Samuel was likely to meet. His plans would amaze him he said. He would not be disappointed if only he would allow Rutenberg to explore the land.

Next on his list was Chaim Weizmann. He knew that he would have to gain his support if he was to get any further. He had not forgotten his unhappy experiences with him in 1914 when he had tried to gain his support in London for the formation of a Jewish Brigade to fight with the British against Germany and the Turks. The brash Rutenberg had disturbed the careful, diplomatic Weizmann who was then studiously wooing the British government to grant him the Zionists' case for Palestine. Rutenberg could so easily have muddied the waters by pressing for a Jewish brigade at a delicate time. So now, in 1919, he had to tread more carefully.

He was not an integral part of Weizmann's team but he was there in the side-lines and knew all the members. He made his play with each of them in turn.

Weizmann was, of course, suspicious but there was no denying that Rutenberg was a remarkably experienced and effective engineer with good ideas about how electricity might be generated from waterpower.

Weizmann, flushed with his success at convincing the leaders of the Great Powers to adopt Balfour's Declaration, could afford to be almost pleasant with Rutenberg. He smiled benignly as he sought more details of Rutenberg's plans. He had, of course, heard something of them. Few in Paris had not, but he needed to know more. Pinchas, in an uncharacteristically conciliatory mood, congratulated Weizmann on the successful outcome of his meeting with the Conference Committee, but knew he had to convince him. He presented his plans in a calm and considered way with little of his natural brashness in evidence and Weizmann softened.

Figure 14: Council of 'Big Four'. David Lloyd George, Vittorio Emanuele Orlando, Georges Clemenceau and Woodrow Wilson, (from left)

Perhaps he should give him a chance to see what he can make of it. He would soon know if he was just bluster and wind.

The stage was set. The 'Big Four' leaders (America, Britain, France and Italy) had agreed to support the Palestine Mandate and the place of the Jews within it (*Fig. 14*). The desperate need for the long-neglected land to be developed was obvious and a supply of electricity was clearly necessary. Rutenberg and his proposal came at the perfect moment and when it was agreed that the land of Palestine should be explored to assess the suitability of its waters for hydro-electric generation, he was the obvious man to lead it.

But first there was the complication that Palestine was still under military rule, its status as a British Mandated territory had not yet received final international approval and no Treaty, that might give them some legitimacy, had been reached with the defeated Turks. The Military Administration led by Allenby was far from supportive of the Zionists' aims. Many of his officers were completely unaware of the proposals laid out in Balfour's Declaration. It was hardly publicised in Palestine at the time. They felt that the land was not theirs to offer to anyone. The land was enemy territory under military occupation and as such should be maintained in the status quo. Claims for immigration and land purchase by the Jews were strongly resisted and the scene was set for constant debate between the army in situ, the Foreign Office in London and the negotiators in Paris about what may or may not be permissible. This was during a time when the borders of Palestine had not yet been decided and Britain and France were still mistrustfully discussing their relative Mandatory stakes in the Middle

East. And the Hashomite leadership, Hussein in Mecca and his son Prince Feisal, had not given up hope of their Middle East Kingdom. Meanwhile the Palestinian Arabs could see the dangers to them in an uncertain future. Although they were in an overwhelming majority of ten to one they felt increasingly vulnerable as they were threatened with a takeover by an ambitious minority. The Zionists did not help. After 2,000 years they were impatiently pressing for the promise of Balfour to be fulfilled. Chaim Weizmann, Head of the Zionist's Organisation, tried hard to contain their zeal but they used every opportunity to parade their ideas of a future Jewish homeland leading to statehood. Little wonder that, in this extremely unstable situation, Arab riots broke out in 1920, just when Rutenberg was busily mapping the potential of the Jordan River to produce hydro-electricity.

The League of Nations was not to give formal approval for another three years. In Paris, Britain's representatives wrestled with the problem of how they could start serious exploration of a land for which it had not yet been given any legitimate responsibilities.

Here is where Rutenberg presented an obvious solution.

Why not obviate this little problem by dispatching an unofficial expert group and not one sponsored by the Government? And of course, he should lead it.

That did not prevent delays for the Russian Rutenberg being given the necessary travel visa to a territory under British military control. It was only awarded in October 1919. By then he had lost patience and was already in Palestine having travelled there under his own steam without a visa, passing across borders with a mixture of audacity and inventiveness.

Once there he immediately set about exploring the terrain, riding back and forth on horseback across the Jordan valley. Armed and escorted by a military force he toured the ill-defined areas of north and north-eastern Palestine with his British team. Here he was doing what he craved most; to be a man of action, engaged in a vision of the future.

The Jordan River with its tributaries was his main focus. His grand plan was to supply electricity to the whole of Mandatory Palestine, on both sides of the Jordan, and to do so he would need as much water flow as he could get. He lost no opportunity in impressing anyone he could with his ideas.

Within three months of arriving in Palestine, he had lobbied the Chief Administrator of the British Military Occupying Force, General L B Bols and when Herbert Samuel visited early in 1920, he too was subject to the Rutenberg treatment. Both urged the Colonial Office to award him the rights to the flow of water from the north. By July 1920 he was able to produce a preliminary but remarkably detailed plan for providing a steady supply of electricity whatever the season, whether during the torrents of spring or trickles of summer. He proposed a series of reservoirs to control the flow of water with new dams to hold it back during times of plenty and release it during times of drought. The first iteration of his plan involved a series of canals parallel to each side of the Jordan River feeding no less than 14 power stations between Lake Kineret and the Dead Sea.

That it was extremely ambitious did not deter him as he stressed the case for as wide a source of water as he could possibly obtain. A power plant at the junction of the Jordan and Yarmouk rivers, just south of Lake Kineret (Lake of Galilee or of Tiberius) was where he focussed his efforts (*Diagram 1*).

It was now that his plan came up against the first huge hurdle. He would need to include the waters of rivers that arose in countries destined to be under the control of other territories; he wanted to join the Litani River in Lebanon to the origins of the Jordan River by canals to cover the five kilometres that separated them, in order to gain the extra water he needed.

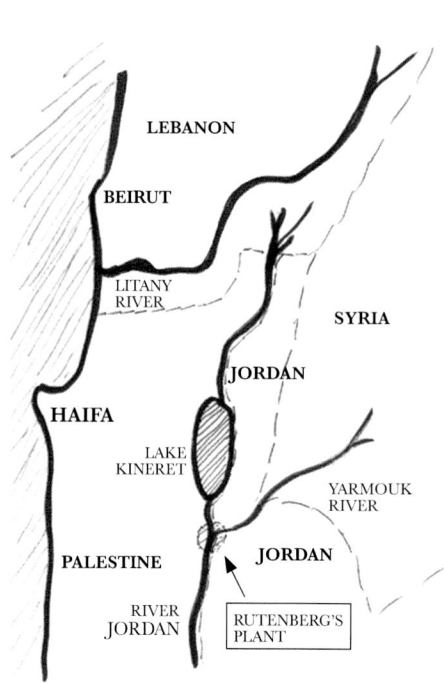

But here was the problem; the Litani arose in Syrian territory, to which the French lay claim, and the Yarmouk arose in what was to become Trans-Jordan after Winston Churchill carved it off from Palestine in 1921. Furthermore, the eastern rim of Lake Kineret was not unambiguously part of British Mandated Palestine. He would have to deal with the French as well as the British Government on that too.

Diagram 1: Site of Rutenberg's proposed power plant at the junction of the Jordan and Yarmouk rivers

Here was where the battle lines were to be drawn between Britain and France and where Weizmann and the Zionists, together with the indomitable Rutenberg, were to set up their camp. This was just one element in the fraught, mistrustful, post-war relations between the French and British and we will return to those later. For the moment he had won the first battle. Samuel was convinced and was even more supportive when Rutenberg revealed that he had secured a promise of £100,000 for his scheme from the Jewish National Fund.

But he was soon to face strong opposition within the Colonial Office, within Parliament and within an extremely hostile press. How he overcame them is the subject of the next chapter.

CHAPTER 9

Facing the opposition

Rutenberg's plans faced opposition in Britain, France and locally in Palestine, and here was the moment, in 1920, when Rutenberg changed his mode of operation from an expert planner of water-engineering projects to a political operator on the international scene. By sheer willpower and determination he managed to overcome most of the problems he encountered and, in so doing, changed the course of history in shaping the future of what was to become the Jewish State. He was very well equipped with the technical skills and knowledge he would require. That was the easy bit. It was the political, diplomatic, legal, cultural and ideological hurdles he would have to surmount that were to cause the most difficulties. These were to keep him fully occupied for many years beyond 1920 as he made the case wherever he could.

Rutenberg's plans were not being made in isolation and we should spend a little time deviating into the many issues facing Britain and its allies as they came to grips with the difficult post-war years.

These, and local distractions in Palestine, had a direct impact on the ways in which he had to adapt and respond.

Weizmann and the Zionists had been successful at the Paris Peace

Conference but the Arabs, represented by Prince Feisal and his father King Hussein, were not. They soon felt that they had been sold down the river by Britain and their disappointment was reflected in their attitude to Rutenberg and his plans.

Back in 1915, King Hussein had been led to believe that if he joined forces with British troops in an armed revolt against the Turks he would be rewarded by Britain with an Arab Empire stretching across most of the Middle East. This agreement formed the basis of the notorious correspondence between Britain's Henry McMahon and King Hussein of the Hejaz that was worded in a characteristically British ambivalent manner. Henry McMahon was High Commissioner in Cairo and writing on behalf of the British Government to King Hussein. The King believed a promise had been made by Britain, in McMahon letters, that most of Syria and Mesopotamia would become part of his kingdom. But although the correspondence has been poured over ever since, its imprecision has allowed different interpretations. The net result was that it was overtaken when the war ended. Much to the chagrin of the Arabs, who believed Britain had reneged on a promise, any apparent agreement was lost. By then Britain and France had agreed to carve up Syria and Mesopotamia between them for their own Mandated Territories, thus storing up much resentment that led to accusations of treachery by the Arabs. These have never entirely disappeared. Britain had to choose between supporting their ally France with its claim on Syria, a claim that Lloyd George had already accepted, and reneging on Hussein's presumptive claim to the same land. France was always going to win.

One of the immediate effects was that King Hussein's son, Prince Faisal, took independent action and declared himself King of Syria in March 1920. He was not to last long and the French evicted him by force on the 24th of July, not long after the Mandates were confirmed by the Great Powers in San Remo. All this was going on while Rutenberg rode the hills.

It was the rejection of Arab wishes that led to many of the problems he faced in gaining acceptance for his plans for electrification in Palestine.

Nineteen twenty was to be an eventful year in the Middle East, and not only for Rutenberg.

Hitherto, leading Palestinian Arab families, so-called 'notables', had been content to be part of a Syrian pan-Arabism and there was little sense of a distinct Palestinian Nationalism. Faisal had even reached an agreement with Weizmann giving the Jews freedom to immigrate into the Palestinian part of what he believed would become his greater Arabian Syria. But the French takeover put an end to aspirations for a pan-Arabism that would have included Palestinian Arabs, and instead, a distinct and separate Palestinian Nationalism began to grow.

Diagram 2: Disputed borders of Palestine, 1920s

Two new hurdles to Rutenberg's plans were being erected; Palestinian Arab resentment with a rise in their own nationalistic desires; and a new border, as yet to be determined, between French Syria and British Palestine, across which the waters so vital to his hydro-electric plans were to flow (*Diagram 2*).

It was the hard-fought arguments over this contentious border, which moved back and forth between the separate Mandated Territories, that caused much delay to Rutenberg's plans. The border was debated in Paris in 1919, at the San Remo Conference in April 1920 and in Geneva at the League of Nations in 1922 and it was several years before it was finally agreed.

The Arabs of Palestine were increasingly restive against the Jews and the British Administration. By May of 1921 they were in open revolt and rioting saw Jewish deaths and destruction of property. Rutenberg took up arms, engaging with the new Jewish self-defence militia and was soon put in charge of the Tel Aviv branch of the Haganah, (Jewish militia). He was re-united with his old comrade Ze'ev Jabotinsky and now he was primed to help protect Jewish interests by force if necessary. He was doing so while heavily engaged in his hydro-electric plans and was in close discussions with the newly arrived High Commissioner, Herbert Samuel.

A Commission of Inquiry into the riots, the Haycraft Report, concluded that it was all the fault of the Jews who were angering the Arabs by immigrating into Palestine and taking over their land. Haycraft seems to have forgotten that it was the British Government's policy based on the Balfour Declaration that had promoted just this immigration and land development. It was little surprise then that his Report was lost as Samuel's Civil Administration took over from the Military Administration.

Strangely the riots worked in favour of Rutenberg's scheme when Colonial Office officials saw investment in Palestinian infrastructure as benefitting Arabs as well as Jews. They optimistically postulated that relationships would be improved and the tendency to riots would fall as a result of the improved infrastructure created by Jewish investment and enterprise. And electrification was seen as a key building block in that fanciful vision. Herbert Samuel was also favourably disposed to a similar view and continued to press the case.

These were the shifting sands that formed the background against which Rutenberg had to act; the San Remo Conference where decisions were being made about the future of the Middle East, the French takeover of Syria with the expulsion of Faisal, and the Arab riots in Palestine of May 1921 were all in the mix. We will come shortly to another significant event in 1921, the creation by Churchill of two new countries (Iraq and Trans-Jordan).

The list of problematic barriers Rutenberg faced would have led a lesser person to depressed inaction. He had to overcome the doubtful officialdom of the Foreign Office and the Colonial Office; a British Media on the warpath against not only his scheme and him personally but also against the idea of a Jewish Palestine; and an unfriendly British Parliament. The French were resistant to his requests for water to flow from their Mandated Territory in the north; his bid for funds from American philanthropists would prove troublesome, and he faced difficulties when he tried to purchase equipment from Germany.

He was, however, fortunate that the case he made did have the support of a series of officials and Ministers in the British Government. Herbert Samuel had been convinced well before he became High Commissioner and he was even more so now. He and others were clear that a ready supply of water to an otherwise parched Palestine was vital not only for irrigation and agriculture, but also to generate the electricity needed for industrialization, lighting, heating, refrigeration and, critically, for the railways. Rutenberg was adamant too that his scheme would increase employment and encourage the immigration and necessary investment from abroad. Only in this way would Britain gain the advantages of a successful, productive country able to stand on its own two feet with minimal Government expense.

Winston Churchill came fully on board once he had met Pinchas Rutenberg in Jerusalem in March 1921. Churchill had been appointed Colonial Secretary in February 1921 and had just drawn his straight lines in the sand creating two new countries, Trans-Jordan and Iraq. Churchill was tasked with reducing expenditure in the Middle East and he used the opportunity to offer Prince Faisal and his brother, Abdullah, some belated recompense for supporting Britain during the war. It was at a meeting in Cairo that Churchill divided off Trans-Jordan from Palestine, made Abdullah the Emir, and began the process of withdrawing expensive troops from there and its neighbour, the newly created Iraq. He knew that placing Prince Abdullah on the throne in Trans-Jordan would disturb the French who could not abide the Hashomite family and their pretensions for Syria. He knew too that it did not make it any easier for Britain to reach a deal with the French on the border issue. But none of that deterred him when he met Rutenberg in Jerusalem.

It was this meeting that was critical in moving Rutenberg's plans forward.

Churchill had just had a difficult conversation with representatives of the Arabs who were pressing him to reverse Britain's policy based on Balfour's Declaration. He resisted their claims, pointing out with some irritation that it was not his prerogative to change Government policy. It was with some relief that he now met someone offering a positive version of the future. He and Rutenberg hit it off immediately. Both were resourceful men of action, full of enthusiasm and a lack of inhibitions. Each was quick to reach decisions and ready to overcome any opposition. Churchill was not unaware of Rutenberg's proposals to develop hydro-electricity. His Parliamentary Secretary, Sir John Shuckburgh, had already raised it with him, but he needed to be convinced.

Their conversation must have been interesting.

Rutenberg made no bones about the case he presented. He would make a Palestinian desert into a thriving, productive agricultural and industrial country of which Britain would be proud. And if that was not enough inducement, it would not be at Britain's cost. Churchill was in the process of reducing costs in the Middle East by withdrawing troops and was clearly piqued. Rutenberg pressed him, as a quid pro quo to ensure that the waters he would need to flow in the Jordan required the agreement of the French in their territory to the north. The whole future of this ambitious scheme depended on it. Or so he said.

He then gave Churchill a copy of his impressively detailed plan for the Jordan River project. Churchill left the meeting in no doubt about Rutenberg's abilities and enthusiasm. Here was a man capable of fulfilling his proposals and a year later, in Parliament, Churchill was able to pull Rutenberg's plan out of the fire when it was in jeopardy.

We now come to the critical nine months between April 1921 and January 1922 when Rutenberg went into overdrive as he tried to overcome all opposition to his plans.

This was to be the most hazardous part of his plan; convincing the British Government to award him the concession to carry out the work.

Concessions to non-Governmental bodies were a time-honoured way for Britain to exert influence in their Colonies without having to pay for them. But in this instance, officials in the Colonial Office were less than convinced that Rutenberg was the person to whom they should grant the concession he was seeking. Furthermore, it all seemed premature, and probably illegal, before the Mandate had been approved by the League of Nations. Other applications from two British firms, Vickers and Century Building, were apparently turned down for just that reason. It was unclear too, what the industrial uses might be for all the electrical output Rutenberg was now proposing. And how was it to be funded? Overall, there was a sense that official commitment to the Zionist's dream was less than firm and Rutenberg's past history as a Russian revolutionary was regarded as not conducive to confidence. Here was the basis of the worries being expressed by Colonial Office officials.

Equally, there was the growing sense in Parliament that the whole Zionist enterprise had been a huge mistake.

In April he submitted his plans to the High Commissioner and in July he met Colonial Office officials in London. He had several official meetings including one with an Arab delegation. This was followed by a further series of journeys, first home to Jerusalem then back to London in December and on to Berlin before a fund-raising trip to America at the end of January 1922. Exhausting trips by sea, none without controversy and despite the Government not giving him the *laissez passe* that would have eased his passage. In vain did he point out how much helpful intelligence he had passed on to the British army chiefs when he was holed up in Odessa in early 1919. Despite all the resistance at every stage and after much heated discussion he gained a signed approval for his hydro-electric plan in September. How did he manage it?

CHAPTER 10

Government antagonism

A draft concession document, written by Herbert Samuel with Rutenberg's help, was submitted to the Colonial Office in May 1921. It made a maximal case and included many proposals that had no hope of being accepted by officials in London. Suggestions that any profits from the scheme should be tax-free, that customs duty on equipment should be waived and that exclusive rights should be granted to the concession holder provoked immediate opposition.

There was a hint too that some officials entertained the belief that, as huge profits were to be gained by Rutenberg, he should be paying the Government for the privilege of being granted a concession.

Other problems were raised. Too few details about the charges to customers, what was to happen to any profits, what measures would be taken to prevent water pollution and the whole problem of acquisition of land when the recent riots had clearly shown how much local opposition there was to any Zionist enterprise. A particular bone of contention was his bid for 50,000 dunam of land near the Jordan River to accommodate his workforce.

He was at a loss to understand why the High Commissioner could not see the economic advantages of him being able to house his own workers there, and for them to be able to protect themselves without the need for the expensive police force the Administration would have to provide. To no avail, as by now the disposal of land was hotly contested by the Arabs in the wake of the Haycraft Report on the riots. The Colonial Office and Herbert Samuel refused point blank to the request; at least for then.

Then there were the questions of whether the French would allow the use of water arising in their territory and what exactly was the role of the Zionist organisation? We will return to these two significant issues later, but they were of less concern to British officials than the more immediate worries.

Finally, we have Curzon's concern at the Foreign Office, about the prospect that the award of a concession for a commercial enterprise might open the door to American oil speculators. The latter were keen to encroach on Britain's Middle East interests and Foreign Secretary Curzon needed reassurance that Rutenberg was not creating an unwanted precedent. That, at least, was achieved by some clever wording by the High Commissioner of the limitations to be placed on external investment.

Officials took the usual route of setting up expert committees to provide advice on each of the economic, legal and technical aspects of the case. In the end however, it was the political case that determined the outcome.

Rutenberg was in London setting out his stall in person in the first of his series of international trips.

On the 5th of July 1921, he and his lawyer, Harry Nathan, laid out his plans to a team from the Middle East Department of the Colonial Office. Nathan had become a key figure in the negotiations (*Fig. 15*). A partner in the firm of Oppenheimer and Nathan, he had been a major in the World War and later became deeply concerned with leading philanthropists and business leaders critical to Rutenberg's fund-raising efforts. He was heavily involved in drafting commercial legislation for export to Palestine and in 1929 became a Liberal Member of Parliament for East London. Later, he was elected as a Labour Member of Parliament before being elevated to a Peerage as Lord Nathan. Gerard Clausen and Roland Vernon, two Junior officials in the Middle East Department of the Colonial Office, were unhappy and minuted their concerns. Feeling that Arab objections were too strong, they became particularly incensed when Rutenberg jumped the gun and raised the electrification of the railways as a prime objective for which the Government should pay. Now Vernon had reluctantly agreed to meet him in a round table discussion.

Rutenberg, giving the impression of an independent entrepreneur, proved flexible and Vernon and his colleagues in the Colonial Office slowly

Figure 15: Lord Nathan

began to sense that here was a man who could deliver. His negotiating skills were strongly in evidence. During several more meetings Rutenberg dropped many of his original demands and agreed to delay others until later. In deferring his more controversial demands he convinced officials that they should feel more confident in him as someone they could trust to deliver. The need to purchase large amounts of land near the Jordan River to protect his many workers was to be left over for the moment. He could come back to it as and when the time was ripe and the same was true of his demands for funding for the railway plan. He knew it was not immediately essential and he pinned his hopes on simply gaining permission to begin.

It is worth examining how and why he was able to circumnavigate an issue on which he had placed so much emphasis at the outset. He had calculated that an electrified railway would be necessary to provide a viable commercial outlet for the huge amount of electricity he would generate from the Jordan River power plant.

That the railway system needed upgrading was certain and it was inevitable that he would light on it as a solution. The network was made up of three different railway lines each with a different gauge from the others, with all trains run on coal. He made the case in a detailed 14-page plan in which he pointed out both the desirability of the scheme, a change from expensive and inefficient coal to a cheaper and efficient alternative, plus a necessary outlet for much of the electricity he would generate. He went about developing his case in great detail, collecting huge amounts of technical and financial data including a survey of electrified railways in Europe and America.

As in India, a well-functioning rail system was of critical strategic and military importance to a colonial power and Rutenberg's well worked out plans for Palestine might have been thought to be a valuable asset to Britain in their Mandated Territory. He fondly imagined that the British Government would be happy to pay for such an important asset. The line between Jaffa and Jerusalem passed through Lydda where Britain had placed its airport. It also provided an important junction with a line running North and South (*Diagram 3*). But the Jaffa-Jerusalem line had belonged to the French and, with the defeat of the Turks, it was now returned to their ownership. Rutenberg proposed that it should be bought by Britain and then electrified (*Fig. 16*).

There followed a prolonged series of debates that finally saw Rutenberg disappointed. Much later Britain did purchase the line for £600,000 but were

Diagram 3: Map of railways of Palestine, circa 1920s

unwilling to fund Rutenberg to develop and run it despite the strong support he had obtained from the British Institute of Electrical Engineers, the English Electric Company and the electric company, Westinghouse. He had surreptitiously approached the engineering company, Vickers Ltd, to seek a tender for electrical equipment. He had the strong support, too, of Colonel Holmes, Director of Palestine Railways and Sir John Snell, Head of the Electricity Commission. 'I do not recollect to have seen any scheme which has been more carefully prepared. …the whole conception is of a most statesmanlike character,' Snell wrote to Herbert Samuel on 7th March 1921. Rutenberg had been nothing if not thorough.

All this was much to the chagrin of Gerard Clausen in the Colonial Office who was incensed that Rutenberg had jumped the gun in approaching engineering companies without their say-so.

Figure 16: Railway carriage at site of Jaffa station

And the plan was far too expensive. Rutenberg had sought a sum of £250,000 plus a promise of £40,000 a year from the Government to run it thereafter. Far too much came the reply and Rutenberg was faced with the problem that, if the Government was unwilling to help, his whole electrification plan would be in jeopardy without the railways; or so it seemed. Colonial Office officials were adamant that if he wanted the railway he could buy it himself.

A final nail in the coffin of the railway arose at a meeting held on 23rd August when the consulting engineer, Preece, of Preece, Cardew and Rider, advised that the proposal could not be profitable. Coal was cheap and oil was just around the corner and likely to be more economic. Furthermore, the cost of purchase of the Jaffa-Jerusalem railway from the French was prohibitive, even though it was eventually paid. The price for the Government was clearly becoming far too high unless Rutenberg covered it himself.

However, there is more than a hint that it was not simply a matter of economics and political bias that crept in. Colonial Office reluctance to support a bid from an, as yet untested, lone businessman played a part. The Government were already wary of giving away too much control to this blustering Russian with bad manners. They delayed and delayed for four or more years and never did give him the railway commission.

Given the impasse, it was then that Rutenberg showed a shrewd sense of the art of the possible. Rather than insisting, he decided not to pursue the railway scheme for the moment. Leaving it out of the agreement gave him room to come back to it later as and when the time might be more favourable. Conditions for an electrified railway never did become favourable for Rutenberg although he did gain an agreement that the Government might be willing to take up £36,000 worth of electricity if electrified railways were running in three years' time. They were not.

We now know that by the time the Jordan River plan came to fruition some nine years later, it was no longer dependent on a railway scheme that never materialized. But at the time, it created much angst for Rutenberg and it certainly proved a missed opportunity for Britain. It was not until almost a hundred years later that Israel electrified its line between Jerusalem and Tel Aviv.

CHAPTER 11

Negotiating tactics

While in London, Rutenberg took the opportunity to meet a Muslim-Christian Delegation from Palestine and invited them to his hotel. They clearly had more trust in him than in Weizmann whom they never agreed to meet. He believed that their conversations were friendly as he had shown his willingness to involve the Arabs, if they so wished, in the investment, in the rewards and in the workforce of his hydro-electric plan. It soon became clear that the Delegation would have nothing to do with the scheme. A letter in the name of the leader of the Delegation, Musa Kassem al-Husseini, was uncompromising. 'We regret that we are unable to give our views on your matter prior to the final resolution of policy by the government of Eretz Yisroel (in other words, until the Balfour Declaration was annulled). Although 'nothing would give us greater pleasure than industries contributing to the wellbeing and prosperity of EY… we should be given the opportunity to take these projects on for ourselves.' This did not stop Rutenberg painting an encouraging picture of his meeting in his later attempts to persuade Samuel that the Arabs would eventually come round given enough time. Despite the apparent bonhomie at their meeting, Sir John Shuckburgh at the Colonial Office well knew that, 'The Arabs in London are not representative and, in any event, will never accept Rutenberg's plans'.

Meanwhile he was desperate to get on and start his scheme. He was pressing everyone he could to sign the agreement. Weizmann, Shuckburgh, Samuel and officials received a barrage of not always polite correspondence. He even threatened to travel to Scotland to challenge Churchill who had retreated there to mourn the deaths of his mother and young daughter. Shuckburgh warned him off such a dangerous idea. But by now his patience was wearing thin and he only reluctantly held back.

Rutenberg was not alone in wanting to see some progress. Weizmann was away at the Zionist Congress in Carlsbad and having a hard time convincing the attendees that developments in the promised land had not stalled. His bete noir, Ze'ev Jabotinsky, was making fiery speeches undermining Weizmann whose position was increasingly at risk. Then there was an unedifying spat with Louis Brandeis that did not help. Brandeis, the American Supreme Court Justice, had considerable influence not only with the American Jewish Community but also with the government there. He supported a complete change in Zionist policies and Weizmann desperately needed some signs of progress. If he could point to a successful concession for Rutenberg's hydro-electric plan he would gain some welcome relief.

Sir John Shuckburgh, Churchill's Assistant Under Secretary of State, was also increasingly anxious to see progress. He was convinced by Rutenberg's argument that the Arabs would see the light with the promise of increased prosperity that electrification would bring to all sections of society. Britain desperately needed a more peaceful Palestine and Rutenberg was offering a way in which it might be possible to mitigate the Arab unrest. It was Shuckburgh who rode over the arguments of officials who were worried about economic and technical concerns by pointing out the political advantages.

Shuckburgh was realistic and, as a friend of the Zionists, he suggested that Rutenberg's scheme was the most obvious and practical way in which the Government could fulfil the responsibilities it had entered into in the Balfour Declaration. Hubert Young in the Colonial Office was of a similar mind and believed that the Arabs would come on board once they saw the benefits from all the investment and development paid for with Jewish money. 'I really believe that the real hope lies in Rutenberg, for whom I have a high regard, and I believe we must soak up a certain amount of unpleasantness for the sole purpose of hastening our progress and bringing his project to fruition as quickly as possible', he wrote in July to Wyndam-Deedes, Chief Secretary to the High Commissioner in Palestine. Young was anxious to see the deal over the line before he and Vernon visited Palestine in October.

Herbert Samuel was also keen to see the plan signed off, but he was in a difficult position from which he had to be helped to extricate himself. For him as High Commissioner he had to appear unbiased and fair to both Arabs and Jews. He wanted to see progress but felt he should obtain Arab approval first. Perhaps the Advisory Council in Palestine would approve it, or possibly the Muslim-Christian Delegation in London might agree?

In a final flourish Shuckburgh telegrammed Samuel on the 9th of September with a message, endorsed by Churchill, to press him to sign the agreement with Rutenberg without Arab approval on the grounds that there would be enough time to gain their support when the concession came to be activated. Samuel needed more reassurance and this came in a secret letter, signed by Rutenberg, to be filed in the Colonial Office unless and until needed. 'I would like to clarify that if there is real opposition (by the Arabs) it will not be possible … to realise the necessary capital to implement the project and, therefore, in that case I will have to abandon the project, or alternatively, adjust its conditions … to answer the demands of local opposition.' A hostage to fortune, but one that demonstrated Rutenberg's pragmatic approach and a genuine desire to reach agreement with the Arabs. Samuel tried to square the circle by putting an announcement in the press instead of facing the Arabs directly with a request for approval and that, in the end, was enough. The Agreement was signed on September 29th 1921, about six months after Rutenberg had first put it forward (*Fig. 17*).

Figure 17: A Half-Promised Land. Cartoon from 'Punch' (7th June 1922)

Of course, it was not the full-throated roar of approval that Rutenberg desired but it was a good enough, if partial, offer that allowed him to begin. Naturally, it had been changed considerably by then. Any profits greater than 10% were to be ploughed back into development and land acquisition, and the railway plan was put on the back burner. And the major scheme on the Jordan River would have to wait until he had proved himself in a smaller scheme based on the Auja (Yarkon) River near to Jaffa.

The much larger Jordan River plan was accepted but only in principle. Although Government officials recognised that the initial agreement for a much smaller scheme would open the door for the Jordan River proposal, they consoled themselves with the knowledge that it would take much more time and further discussion. For the Government it offered the opportunity to test Rutenberg's capacity to deliver while for Rutenberg it raised the prospects for his much bigger plans.

Now he had to set up his Company within two years, that is by September 1923, and to raise commitments for a million pounds with £200,000 up front. The smaller power plant on the Auja River was a welcome start. This, at last, allowed him to return to Jerusalem in some triumph. But even then, clouds were gathering.

Opposition by the Arabs was becoming organised and their voice was being heard in the British press and in Parliament. Criticism was heard not only against Rutenberg personally and his electrification scheme, but increasingly against the idea of a Jewish homeland. Then there was an additional problem with his Auja River programme. He belatedly recognised that there was never going to be sufficient water flowing down this river to generate enough power to make it worthwhile. We will come back to how he solved these problems with a mixture of innovative thinking and sheer audacity.

But first he faced the need to raise some money.

CHAPTER 12

Raising funds

It was in America and London where he focussed his fund-raising efforts. He set off to America in December 1921, via London and Berlin. His Berlin adventure can wait but it was in America wher he found himself in a quagmire. Arriving there at the end of January 1922, he started with his characteristic energy and enthusiasm but was immediately faced with a battle within the Jewish community and between American and British Jewish organisations. He had to have the funding by September 1923 if he was to meet the deadline, but everywhere he tried he came across objections. He complained that while everyone he met was charming and convinced of the enormous value of his electrification plans, no-one was willing to offer any material support. As the Americans disappeared behind a wall of questions and obscurantism, he failed to grasp why they could not see the enormous value of his project.

Figure 18: Louis Brandeis, Supreme Court Justice of America

Supreme Court Justice Louis Brandeis was an interesting case (*Fig. 18*). He certainly favoured individual investment in specific business deals in a land that would provide commercial opportunities. It might be thought he would be early in his support, but he and his colleagues were in no hurry. They could not understand Rutenberg's urgency and were making demands that Rutenberg was unable or unwilling to meet. Pressing for more financial and technical details than he was willing to provide, they demanded control over the management board. They might provide 50% of the funds but in return they would need 50% of the seats on his board. Part of the problem may have been that Rutenberg's project was not seen as a secure investment with anything like guaranteed profit and the hard-nosed Americans were far from convinced that he could deliver. But there was a more significant sticking point and that was American suspicions of the role of Weizmann and his British Zionists. They knew that Weizmann believed that funds should be raised for non-specific purposes to support the economic and demographic base for the new State. Brandeis and co., on the other hand, felt strongly that funds should only be sought for specific commercial and industrial developments in a country operating as a cultural and spiritual centre rather than the Homeland. Furthermore, they wanted to know that the British Government would not be gaining any commercial bencfits to the disadvantage of America.

They were suspicious too, of British financiers whom they thought would gain preferential treatment in the purchase of equipment. Here was the sticking point; they wanted nothing to do with Britain's or the Zionists' role in influencing the future of Palestine. Rutenberg was stuck in the middle. Brandeis and Weizmann parted company as the former thought that the time for the latter's international lobbying was over. Their animosity became increasingly personal and very counterproductive.

Rutenberg despaired of gaining support from either of these groups, pulling in different directions, and decided to stir things up by seeking support from non-Jewish Wall Street investors. But it was his threat to expose the divisions within the Jewish community by going directly to the public that caused more difficulties.

Finally, the Z.O. coughed up £50,000 and Keren HaYesod, another £53,000. Both organisations, in Britain, were desperate not to expose Jewish supporters to damaging ridicule.

By the time he left for London he had wasted much of 1922 in America and, frustratingly, he was no further forward.

American resistance to accepting British influence on his new company proved too much for him and, in any event, he was much more attracted to British backers whom he knew had more political influence on their Government and the Mandatory Authority.

Meanwhile, in London, the Zionist Organisation and Weizmann were pulling in another direction. They too were in no hurry and were also pressing for 50% of the seats on the management committee. If he behaved himself, they would allow Rutenberg a seat for himself. He was incensed by what he saw as a brazen attempt to usurp him.

He was never going to cede ultimate control to the Americans, the British or Weizmann and the Zionists and he now had to struggle his way out from under their conflicting claims on what he saw as his baby.

It is to his relationship with Weizmann that we must now turn (*Fig. 19*). He certainly needed the support of the Zionist Organisation to demonstrate his legitimacy to the Government.

He insisted that the Z.O. be formally recognised in the agreement he had already signed in London, but the last thing he needed was for them to be able to interfere with his plans. He was clear that he wanted no political involvement or interference in what was going to be a strictly commercial venture. To him it could not possibly be run effectively in any other way. Not unreasonably, he thought he would keep Weizmann at a distance, believing that an overtly political body should not be involved in management. Weizmann did not see it that way and was incensed by Rutenberg's efforts to side-line him. He could not forget that it was he who had been instrumental in ensuring that Rutenberg was appointed to lead the exploration of the Jordan River in 1919 and had arranged a grant of £12,500 from the Z.O. for him to do so. After all, he suggested, it was

Figure 19: Chaim Weizmann

he who had introduced Rutenberg to the Colonial Office. According to him, Rutenberg had been given the concession as a representative of the Z.O. and, as a result, the Z.O. should have a half share and a decisive voice in the Company. Now, he said, Rutenberg was wriggling out of it in an unforgivable breach of trust. He then tried to deny Rutenberg any legitimate right to portray the scheme as his own. The fact that the Z.O. could not afford to put enough money into the scheme to warrant such an influential part was something he ignored. However, he went off beam when he suggested that Rutenberg was treating the scheme purely as a business venture and in doing so did not have the interests of the nation at heart. He put it about that Rutenberg would use the profits for his own personal gain and not for the good of the country.

Rutenberg was certainly now acting as an entrepreneur but the accusation that he did not care for the future of the Palestinian homeland, or that he did not contribute to it, was far from the mark. Others on the Zionist executive tried to calm Weizmann down, but his anger was not to be assuaged. He had formed an ill opinion of the brash Rutenberg back in 1914 and now he had even more reason to lose faith in a man whom he believed had reneged on promises and betrayed his trust. Needless to say, Rutenberg could not accept the conditions that Weizmann laid out and their relationship never recovered. From now on Rutenberg did his best to keep the Z.O. out of the picture by rarely reporting progress to them, and Weizmann continued to fume at meetings of the Z.O.

However, Weizmann was not the only one who was suspicious of Rutenberg's motives. It was a matter that also taxed the

Colonial Office during their deliberations at the time, and continued to reverberate over the years.

Time was running out and Rutenberg's mental health was suffering. He was almost at the end of his tether when he re-visited London in July 1922 and called a meeting of interested parties to try yet again to hammer out a deal. Promises of funding were made and places on the management board offered in proportion to the amount invested by each. It soon became obvious that none of these financial agreements would survive.

The adverse reaction in the British press and Parliament put pressure on Rutenberg to include a clause in the constitution of his company to the effect that purchase of equipment should be restricted to British sources. Those on whom he was so dependent were key political players and he could not safely ignore them. Agreeing to give British manufacturers preferential treatment was a form of political bribery and it was completely unacceptable to the Americans. In a morass of recrimination between the Americans and the British all was lost. Even two years later, a tentative offer of $200,000 by the American Palestine Development Corporation (now the Palestine Economic Corporation) fell by the wayside. Rutenberg had reacted by writing blunt and abrasive letters that he wisely did not send. Not his best or most diplomatic moment but he was beginning to lose what little patience he may have ever possessed. In the end the Americans failed to provide any of the funds for the electrification of Palestine.

By late 1922 Rutenberg was no further forward and his deadline was approaching.

The toll taken on Rutenberg must have been enormous. His mental health deteriorated and the manic, brutal tone of the letters he was firing off were evidence of a man under considerable strain. He let it be known that he could not carry on and would be standing down as leader of the electrification scheme once it was off the ground. Disaster threatened as it was widely recognised that, despite his aggressive, uncompromising personality, without him the enterprise would fail. And, since the whole future development of the Jewish homeland seemed dependent on Rutenberg's electrification scheme, his withdrawal would cause untold damage. His threat, for that is what it appeared at the time, was effective in encouraging some movement in raising the funds, although not from America.

That he survived and was able to continue with increased enthusiasm reveals a character with some reserves and resilience.

While no-one was willing to take the blame for failure, he decided to avoid both the Zionists and the Americans to whom he was writing vitriolic letters. He would go directly to private and other investors. Hitherto he had been unsuccessful in his efforts to work on the reticent Baron Rothschild in Paris but now he managed to gain his attention. If he could persuade others, the Baron might join in, to the tune of £250,000. As the September 1923 deadline neared, the Baron Rothschild finally offered his support through his intermediaries, the two Polak brothers who were given seats on the Management Board.

Others followed. A Russian expat oil baron in London, Michael Nasatissin, was an early investor as were an Egyptian

Jewish group led by Aaron Menashe and the industrialist Alfred Mond (later Lord Melchett) (*Fig. 20*). With his earlier awards from the Keren Hayosed and the Zionists, and a smaller contribution from Bank Hapoalim, he now had £225,000 to start the project on the Auja River. He still had to raise his million pounds for the larger Jordan River programme but for that he had a little more time and meanwhile he was able to set up his Electricity Company and its Board of Management.

Naturally there were some legal niceties to be overcome. He still needed to raise a million pounds and in order for his underwriters in London to agree to underwrite shares in his Palestine Electric Company it would need to be registered in London. He had registered his Company in Palestine but that was of little value since there was to be no stock exchange in Palestine until 1935. He was now faced with a catch 22 situation in which the conditions of the Mandate precluded a Palestinian company from having a branch register in the UK. It would be a prohibited act of discrimination against other states. Confusing, to say the least. Corresponding with the Attorney General and High Commissioner in Palestine and the Undersecretary for the Colonies in London got

Figure 20: Lord Melchett (Alfred Mond), financial supporter of Rutenberg

him nowhere. An ingenious solution, discovered by an official in the Colonial Office, involved the High Commissioner being given the discretion to approve the creation of branch registers under certain conditions. Another sleight of hand saw Orders in Council drafted without having to seek the approval of the Foreign Office and, with the formation of branch registers in both London and Palestine, Rutenberg had his access to the London stock market.

He was now in the hunt for a million pounds and he spent the next three years achieving it by a combination of his powers of persuasion and friends in high places. To do so he jettisoned ideas of ever gaining any support from the Zionist organizations or American players. He focussed on British industrialists and, somewhat surprisingly, the British Government. He got into bed first with the British General Electric Company. It's Chairman, Sir Hugo Hirst, arranged for an investment of £250,000. Although Jewish he was never keen on visiting Palestine and regarded the investment purely as a business proposition that promised dividends. He saw the future development of the land as an important strategic venture for Britain but, whatever his reasons, the involvement of GEC was viewed as highly significant in London. It certainly encouraged others who soon joined. Sir Alfred Mond (Lord Melchett) had been an early supporter and investor and soon the 'cigarette king', Bernard Baron, owner of Carrera cigarettes, joined with his contributions. He invested £100,000 and in so doing upset Weizmann to whom he had promised even larger amounts that were never delivered.

We now turn to the remarkable events surrounding Rutenberg's audacious bid to the Trade Facilities Commission

(TFC). This was an organisation set up by the Government to provide loans to UK industry to help fight the serious unemployment that existed in Britain after the war. A purely inward facing investment company and, on the face of it, not one that would be open to other countries, whether Colonies or Mandates.

It was here that Rutenberg showed his genius for finding loopholes.

His initial, direct approach was immediately turned down and TFC officials would not even agree to meet him. Never one to give up, he went to his friends in the Colonial Office, meeting Sir John Shuckburgh and the then Minister, Leo Amery. The case he presented was persuasive.

If he was offered a loan, his Electric Company would undertake to purchase all the equipment they needed from British manufacturers. That in turn would automatically improve employment in Britain's factories and his company would then be at the forefront in the battle against unemployment. Impeccable logic! Amery tried to see the flaws in the argument but could not do so and accepted the case. He then wrote to the Chairman of the TFC, Sir William Flender, pressing the idea of a loan of £300,000. Flender, not surprisingly, was suspicious and hesitant. His advisors thought that the future of the hydro-electric scheme was flawed and unlikely to succeed but did not argue against the idea of funding British industry indirectly. Lord Melchett intervened with another argument. Britain should be considering the political implications of support for developments in Palestine.

The Middle East was clearly strategically important to Britain and pressure was mounting to invest in developing the land. Why not get on and do it? Rutenberg may even have oiled the wheels by hinting that his Management Board (at this point they knew little of his approach to the TFC) would need funds from Britain if they were to be induced to buy British goods. Perhaps it was this argument that eventually made the difference.

Finally, Flender reluctantly gave way. He agreed to a loan of £250,000 on condition that Rutenberg accepted a requirement to report on the details of his financial control and, most significantly, to purchase all the equipment he needed from British manufacturers. Rutenberg did not spend much time explaining that he had already purchased equipment from Germany. All that was to cease once he had the TFC funds. The grant that Rutenberg finally gained was sufficient to convince his Management Board to go along with the conditions, albeit with some reluctance. Despite already having bought German equipment, from now on the Board was constrained to buy British.

He now had his funding and equally importantly, the legitimacy for his Electric Company had been confirmed by a grant from a Government Agency, a major industry in the shape of the GEC and several significant high-flying industrialists. The support he had gained from Government Ministers and officials was vital, and the final approbation was his recruitment of Lord Reading to be the first Chairman of his Management Board.

There is little doubt that the strain of those years took its toll on Rutenberg and made him pay a physical and mental price.

Much can be learnt of his personality and character from his behaviour during the time he was negotiating for funds. Firstly, his persistence and determination that made him never give up. When one avenue closed, and there were many that did, he immediately looked for another. When he hit a brick wall he simply stepped back and if there was no way round, he gave way, and accepted new conditions as a temporary position to which he might return later. In giving way to some objections to gain more important points, he deployed the art of the possible with the skill of a businessman. And he never gave up.

It was clear too, to everyone who met him, that he was highly intelligent and mounted his arguments with great skill. He was always well prepared and the cases he presented were coherent, logical and persuasive. Despite an impatience with counterarguments and a tendency to aggressive behaviour that caused upset, he gained respect and even admiration for the strength of his convictions backed up by extensive knowledge. He was capable of upsetting many by his outspoken criticisms, often, but not always, warranted. And he hardly ever minced his words, always deep-voiced, with his strong Russian accent and his formidable stare. He never shied away from firing off outlandish missives aimed at those with whom he disagreed. But equally he was convincing enough to have brought many senior members of the Government over to his points of view. So much so that many were converted to support him and to work on his behalf.

He was also secretive. His history as a revolutionary in Russia may well have contributed to these characteristics. In the midst of delicate negotiations, he had no compunction in avoiding mention of them to his colleagues and associates. He was never happy in explaining what he was doing to supporters and only did so when absolutely essential. He much preferred quiet and secret negotiation to open public discussion. Democratic principles were to him the cause of delay and inaction. He much preferred autocracy, especially in his own hands. This characteristic, present most of his days, led him to stipulate in his will that publicity about his life should be strictly limited. It also led to him being considered untrustworthy by some.

Each of these characteristics remained hardly impaired during the rest of his life, but he needed all his strength of character when, in the 1920s, he became the subject of huge personal criticism in the British press and in Parliament.

CHAPTER 13

Trial by media and parliament

During most of the time that Rutenberg was trying to convince Government officials and Ministers to agree to his concession, the press was mounting a systematic campaign against him. The Government was under increasing pressure not only from the media but also from Parliament. Both were campaigning against the Zionists' aspirations and it was inevitable that Rutenberg would be caught up in the stream of vitriol being poured on them. After all, his plans were seen as the clearest manifestation of the basis for a Jewish State. The Mandate for Palestine had not yet, in early 1922, been confirmed by the League of Nations and voices were raised in Parliament about the whole venture before it was too late. The group of Arab representatives in London during 1921 were lobbying the press and Parliament, urging them to rescind the Balfour Declaration.

Debates in Parliament soon took up the theme and MPs and Peers spoke out strongly, using their privileges not only to castigate Rutenberg but to pour cold water on the promises of Balfour's Declaration.

Lord Northcliffe's press was uniformly antagonistic to Zionism (*Fig. 21*). With a scarcely concealed anti-Semitism, *The Times*,

The Daily Mail and *The Evening Standard* all produced articles decrying the Government for their support for the Jewish homeland in Palestine. Northcliffe had form in pouring scorn on those whom he disliked. His vitriolic attacks on Lord Haldane, Lord Chancellor, in 1915 had resulted in his exclusion from Government when the press grossly misled the public about Haldane's efforts to prevent the war with Germany. Northcliffe now turned his fire-power on Zionism and Rutenberg. He had visited Palestine during his world tour in February 1922 when he was already ill and, some said, beginning to behave irrationally. He met many who convinced him that Britain was badly mistaken for supporting the Zionists. Certainly the Arabs were keen to press their case, but there were many religious Jews who feared that the new influx of Zionists would disturb their relations with the Arabs. One such orthodox Jew, Jacob Israel de Haan, was later assassinated for giving Northcliffe anti-Zionist ammunition. The opinions Northcliffe gained in Palestine must have convinced him to change the tune he had previously played when *The Times* blared 'Palestine for the Jews' at the announcement of Balfour's Declaration in 1917 and

Figure 21: Lord Northcliffe, powerful press baron, pressed the case against Rutenberg

even by May 1921 it was still supportive in an article headed 'Water Power From Jordan. Employment for All'. Now he changed his mind and took to lecturing a group of Zionists at Rishon LeTzion about the relative needs of 60 million Arabs compared with a few hundred thousand Jews. He clearly did not believe it was just or fair to deny the Arabs their right to self-Government.

He left his reporter, Philip Graves, in Palestine and it was Graves who produced a stream of reports for publication in Northcliffe's newspapers.

In the days before television, and the internet, newspapers were a major source of information and Northcliffe covered the field with his *Daily Mail* for the common man and *The Times* for the so-called intelligentsia. There had been little public interest in the Middle East after the war when the focus was on domestic affairs, demobilisation, economic recovery and unemployment. Few knew anything about the Mandate for Palestine and even when, in 1922, the press began their campaign, it was only Parliament and the Government that paid any attention.

For Rutenberg, a man who worked best doing deals behind closed doors, to find himself the subject of newspaper headlines must have been disquieting to say the least. 'German Engines; The Rutenberg Mystery; Russian Monopoly at Work' ran the headline in the *Daily Mail* on the 27th of May 1922. It said it all. Rutenberg, a Russian 'Bolshevik' Jew, was buying equipment from the hated Germans to set up a scheme for his own profit in a far-away land and at the expense of the British taxpayer; what *The Times* called 'The Rutenberg Affair'. He should be stopped by fair means or foul, and dirt was raked up wherever it could be found. Rutenberg was a Russian or even a German, it did not matter much which, he was a Jew, maybe a Bolshevik and probably a murderer. He was going to make huge profits for himself and his foreign investors at the expense of Britain's taxpayers and he was being granted a concession ahead of many other British contenders.

Behind the criticisms of Rutenberg lay the fundamental message of the anti-Zionists; the Government was behaving badly by continuing to support the Jews in their quest for a National Home. Since Rutenberg's plans were seen as a key element in the development of Palestine, the Government should back away from them before the Mandate could be confirmed by the League of Nations.

Rutenberg tried to defend himself when he was interviewed by a reporter from *The Times* while he was fund-raising in New York.

The headline to the report reads, 'Monopoly Details; British Firms Get Preference'. He made a good case. 'Mr Rutenberg informs me', wrote the reporter, that the terms of the concession, 'were defined after lengthy negotiations with the Palestine Government and investigation by the legal and technical experts of the Crown Agents for the Colonies. Dividends up to ten percent will be retained by the company; from ten to fifteen percent they will be divided equally, two and a half percent going to the company, the remaining two and a half percent being devoted to the reduction of rates charged for the current.' Rutenberg reportedly said, 'My whole conception for the undertaking is that of a public utility independent of race. We are not interested in politics. We will cooperate with Jews and Arabs with the view of obtaining the most settled conditions possible without which no commercial undertaking can succeed. When the country is at peace, sufficient electricity will be available and, I believe, industries can at once be established to provide work for large numbers of people. Both Jewish and Arab labour will be employed in the construction and operation of the power houses. I am endeavouring to obtain the services of an Arab engineer to supervise the latter. My concession grants a complete monopoly which is necessary if capital is to be interested in the project.' The reporter added that no decision had been reached as to where orders for machinery will be placed but Mr. Rutenberg has written to the Colonial Office stating that he is willing to pay British firms up to ten percent more than asked by firms of other countries.

In case it had been forgotten, Rutenberg was referred to as 'formerly Chief of Police during the Kerensky administration in Russia'.

It proved embarrassing when it was leaked in London by the Zionist Organisation that he was, in fact, in the process of purchasing his engines from Germany. It should be remembered that this was before he had done his deal with the TFC to buy only British equipment. He was furious at the leak and had to obfuscate at a later interview. All these distractions were the last things he needed while suffering the stress of negotiating for funds from reluctant American Jews.

Now it was Parliament's turn to castigate him. Throughout 1920 and 1921 Peers and MPs had been expressing misgivings about the Mandate and particularly the Zionists and their 'National Home'. Then, in June 1922, the Lords alighted on Pinchas Rutenberg as representing all that was wrong with the Government's proposals.

Lord Islington moved that, 'The Mandate for Palestine in its present form is unacceptable to this House… and that its acceptance by the Council of the League of Nations should be postponed …'.

After a diatribe against the Zionists who were usurping the rights of the Arab population, he used the example of Rutenberg and his plans as an example of the perils of Zionism. 'I have no quarrel with him as an individual, but I say that if his scheme, as we have read in the newspapers, ever were allowed to materialise … It would give to a Jewish syndicate wide powers over the economic, social and industrial conditions of an Arab community, and it would give that power for no less than seventy years. It is about the widest power I have ever read in a concession … and goes to the very heart of the economic and industrial conditions of the country.' He asked how come the Rutenberg concession was granted when other bids were rejected? Other industrialists had sought a concession but were turned down because, they were told, nothing could be entertained until the Mandate was confirmed. If that was so, how did Mr Rutenberg gain his concession? It was 'a deliberate policy of economic preference to the Zionists'.

In vain did Lord Balfour, giving his maiden speech in the Lords, try to stem the tide of opposition. His defence of the Jews and their desire for a National Home was masterly but ultimately unsuccessful. The Mandatory system 'was not sprung upon the League of Nations, and, before the League of Nations came into existence it was not sprung upon the Powers that met together in Paris etc. It was accepted in America, it was accepted in this country, it was published all over the world, and if ever there was a Declaration which had behind it a general consensus of opinion, I believe it was the Declaration of 1917.' So far as Rutenberg's scheme was concerned, 'Lord Islington is under a great illusion if he thinks that investors are clamouring for opportunities which had been improperly given to the Jews.' He then gave a paean to the Jews. '… their position and their history, their connection with world religion and with world politics, is absolutely unique. There is no parallel to it, there is nothing approaching to a parallel to it, in any other branch of human history. Here we have a small race originally inhabiting a small country, I think about the size of Wales or Belgium, … At no time in its history wielding anything that can be described as material power, sometimes crushed in between great Oriental monarchies, its inhabitants deported, then scattered, then driven out of the country altogether into every part of the world, and yet maintaining a continuity of religious and racial tradition of which we have no parallel elsewhere.' Consider, he asked, how they have been subjected to tyranny and persecution in Europe '… the whole religious organisation of Europe has, from time to time, proved itself guilty of great crimes against this race.' Despite this they have shone in so many fields of the intellect and society and have been able to do so without having any Jewish Home.

All his efforts were to no avail as Peers were not convinced. Lord Sydenham quoted a telegram from an Arab Association in Jaffa strongly rejecting any concession to Rutenberg while Lord Buckmaster discovered from *The Times* that Rutenberg had been engaged in 'a treacherous and cold-blooded murder'. (He had indeed been an accessory to an assassination; see Chapter 4). The public would undoubtedly be exercised about a preferential right being given to a special and favoured race of people.

It was no competition, and when the vote came, there were 60 Peers in favour of the motion that the Mandate should be delayed and only 29 against.

Prime Minister David Lloyd George anxiously called Winston Churchill to do something to stop the revolt. Having worked so hard to reach an agreement with the French and now, in striking distance of League of Nations approval, he needed to stop what he regarded as anti-Semitic rebels in the Lords interfering with his plans. Churchill in the Colonial Office was shaken and knew that the Government would not be able to avoid a full debate in the Commons. It was held two weeks later, on the 4th of July.

Figure 22: Sir Joynson-Hicks M.P. spoke vehemently in the House of Commons against Zionism and Rutenberg. (July 4th 1922)

Sir William Joynson-Hicks opened the attack (*Fig. 22*). His first salvo was the motion, 'That, in the opinion of this House, the Mandate for Palestine, the acceptance of which must involve this country in financial and other responsibilities, should be submitted for the approval of Parliament, and further, that the contracts entered into by the High Commissioner for Palestine with Mr Pinchas Rutenberg should at once be referred to a Select Committee for consideration and report.' He followed this with a long diatribe about how Britain should redeem its pledge to the Arabs made during the war to give them a wide expanse of the Middle East in return for their support in the war against the Turks. The Arabs had been denied their rightful place by a shameful promise to the Jews. He then made his classical statement on antisemitism. 'I have been accused in this House of being an antisemite. All I can say is that some years ago I had a Jew as partner in my firm, and we were the best of friends and worked together in amity.' The phrase 'some of my best friends etc', comes to mind.

He admitted that he had supported the Zionists in 1917 but that was before he became aware of the implications for the Arabs. Now he knew that to proceed with the Mandate would cause a grave injustice to them. He suggested that, with many if not most of the senior officials in the Government of Palestine being Jewish, it was clearly a takeover from which the Arabs were excluded.

He now turned his ire on Rutenberg. How come he had been granted the electrification concession when others were turned away on the grounds that no concessions could be granted until the Mandate was formally adopted? Would there be any advantage to British suppliers of equipment if Rutenberg was free to buy it anywhere in the world? He knew Germany was a possible source. That 'would be a flagrant violation of the Mandatory principle'. Then he was not convinced that Rutenberg's scheme was a sound one. Where is the plan? It seems to have been hidden from view. Were Government experts sent out to investigate? Have they even seen the original scheme?

'I do not wish to make any capital out of the character of Mr. Rutenberg, but I think, quite seriously, I am entitled to say this much, that Great Britain has no right to hand over such vast powers, and such vast possibilities of control over the whole development of Palestine, to a man whose character is at least the subject matter of very grave suspicion.' Here he is, blackening Rutenberg's name by reference to *The Times* newspaper article, 'with regard to his actual connection with a very horrible murder. There ought to be an inquiry into the antecedents of this gentleman who was admittedly a member of the Kerensky Government in Russia, and such an inquiry ought to have been made before the concession was granted.'

That was the burden of Joynson-Hicks' case against Rutenberg and the Mandate itself. He was supported by Sir J Butcher who drew attention to 'some strange terms in the concession' that 'appear to be of a most dangerous character'. These included the extensive monopoly to supply electricity to the whole of Palestine and Trans-Jordan for a period of 70 years. And that period could be extended by the High Commissioner, whoever he or she was in that distant future. How can 'such an amazing power be a requisite?' And how can that be fair to the Arabs? Then there were the dividends to be paid to investors; 6% tax free. Many English companies would rejoice at such a return.

It was Morgan-Jones MP who began a detailed response. The Arabs were not uniformly antipathetic. Remember Prince Feisal's welcome to the Jews at the 1919 Peace Conference, 'We will wish the Jews a hearty welcome home'. He refuted the claim that Jews dominated the Government service in Palestine by quoting figures to show that they were in a minority. And so far as the concession to Rutenberg was concerned, it was an entirely appropriate contract in all respects.

'I have never been able to appreciate the anti-Jewish sentiment which exists in the world, nor do I sympathise with it.'

It was left to Winston Churchill to demolish the case in a remarkable speech full of his characteristic logical argument, facts and humour (*Fig. 23*). One of his very best. He started by saying that 'This is a topic … which lends itself peculiarly well to criticism. When you have Jews, Russians, Bolshevism, Zionism, electrical monopoly, Government concessions, all presented at the same time … something will be found to rile against.'

Figure 23: Winston Churchill, Colonial Office Secretary of State, saved Rutenberg's case in the Commons (July 4th 1922)

There were two issues. Firstly, should the Government keep to its pledge to the Zionists made in 1917; and secondly, are the ways in which the Government goes about fulfilling that pledge appropriate? He was clear that Parliament did not have the freedom now to repudiate promises made during the war. They were supported very widely in Britain and by its Allies and later by the United States' Senate. Many in Parliament who are now raising objections were very supportive at the time. He rubbed it in by quoting from speeches made by Sir W. Joynson-Hicks, by Sir J Butcher and by Lord Sydenham, amongst others, made in 1917. 'You have no right to support public declarations made in the name of the country in the crisis and heat of the War, and then afterwards, when all is cold and prosaic, to turn round and attack the Minister or the Department which is faithfully and laboriously endeavouring to translate these perfervid enthusiasms into the sober, concrete facts of day-to-day administration. I say, in all consistency and reasonable fair play, that does not justify the House of Commons at this stage in repudiating the general Zionist policy. Acting upon this policy would benefit not only the Jews but the Arabs and the whole population.

'I am told that the Arabs would have done it for themselves. Who is going to believe that?' Not in a thousand years, he suggested in words that would be unacceptable today.

He next focussed on Rutenberg's concession with typical bravura. Were there other applicants for the concession? Yes, of course. Two inhabitants of Bethlehem who 'furnished no plans, no estimates, no scheme at all but they indicated that if there were any concessions going, they would very much like to have them'. A British firm applied for exclusive rights at double the rates Rutenberg was now proposing. Contrast this with the 'utmost detail and with considerable backing' with which Rutenberg has put forward his plans. As for the enormous profits he would be making for his foreign shareholders, he gave details of the modest returns that would only accrue after several years. 'The concession provides that after the company has earned 10 per cent, the profits are to be equally divided between them and the Palestinian Government until 15 per cent has been received, and after that the whole profit reverts to the Palestinian Government.' Investors were not queueing up to invest and certainly no non-Jews found it sufficiently attractive to put any money forward. 'Nearly all the money got up to the present time has come from associations of Jewish character, which are almost entirely on a non-profit-making basis. Profit-making, in the ordinary sense, has played no part at all in the driving force …

'I come to Mr. Rutenberg himself. He is a Jew. I cannot deny that. But if you are going to say 'No Israelite may apply' then I hope the House will permit me to confine my attention exclusively to Irish matters.' (Laughter).

As for Rutenberg being a Bolshevist, he demolished the argument by pointing out the anti-Bolshevik activities that he had clearly demonstrated in Petrograd and Odessa. And, yes, he had heard that he had played a part in the murder of a Father Gapon (*Chapter 4*). But then Gapon had it coming. He had been a traitor and agent provocateur, reporting on his comrades to the Russian police. As an aside he mentioned that Rutenberg may have tried to persuade Kerensky to hang Lenin and Trotsky. Music to Churchill's anti-Bolshevik ears. There was amusement when he stated '… it seems to me that he (Rutenberg) has been entirely consistent.'

Having dealt with Rutenberg he finished with the plea that the Zionists should be allowed to continue their invaluable work in developing the land of Palestine for all its inhabitants.

The vote was overwhelming. The 'Ayes' in favour of the Joynson-Hicks motion, 35, the 'Noes' against, 292. Churchill had won the day by a huge margin.

The result was that the Mandate could go unamended for approval by the League of Nations and Rutenberg was in the clear to continue with his plans. The Colonial Office officials were shaken and continued to find reasons to try to delay his programme but the press lost much of their antipathy for the time being.

CHAPTER 14

The Auja (Yarkon) River project

By the end of 1921 Rutenberg had gained his concession from the Government and he had raised the initial funding needed to start the Auja (Yarkon) River project. He was yet to survive the personal attacks by the British press, and the efforts in the following year to prevent him proceeding were yet to be blocked by his friends in Parliament. But two years after arriving in Palestine he had the concession to begin to realise his ambition.

It was then that Rutenberg showed his facility to achieve his ends by changing as the circumstances demanded. And they certainly demanded.

He had already demonstrated his capacity for pushing through technological schemes with the building of the Tiberias-Tzemach road. He needed the road at the southern tip of Lake Kineret for his electrification scheme and convinced the Administration to allow him to build it. Martialling more than 500 labourers from amongst a mixed group of Arabs and Russian, German and Polish immigrants, he had pulled all the right strings and was now on his way to London where he would be needing all his organizational, diplomatic and political skills to get his Auja River generator off the ground.

The original plan depended on the flow of water down the Auja River to generate sufficient electricity to make it a viable proposition.

Here we must delve a little into the technical details of the scheme if only to show how impractical it turned out to be.

As presented by Rutenberg it included the need to raise an old dam by one metre to increase the head of water, and to excavate a 2.6 kilometre canal. With five transformers this was said to be sufficient to generate enough electricity for irrigation, lighting and industry in the Jaffa and Tel Aviv area.

That was the plan that had been passed by the politicians, it had been examined by the lawyers and economists, but only belatedly was it realised that the Government in London needed an engineer's assessment of its technical feasibility.

The engineering consultants, Preece, Cardew and Rider, gave a hurried response a few days before the deadline and were positive about the scheme. It was very technical. Water flow controls were reasonable and the generation of 350 kilowatts of energy was to be expected. There was little to criticise of a scheme that seemed entirely modern. However, there was one major caution which was ignored that proved to have important consequences. Since the engineers were unable to visit, they knew little or nothing of the local situation. It was this weak link between their expert opinion and local knowledge that turned out to be critical.

Churchill telegrammed Samuel on September 1st 1921 informing him of the favourable report from the engineers, and a few days later Rutenberg had his concession for this part of his scheme. The plot now thickens. Although he had persuaded the High Commissioner to offer £25,000 to the Arab council in Jaffa to help them purchase electricity, he now found that the local Arabs were demanding very high prices for the land he needed near the river. This demand may have been true, but he made much of this difficulty as an excuse for him to radically alter his plans. Much more significant was the realisation that the Auja River was, for most of the year, a mere trickle and its flow was hardly ever going to be sufficient to produce the electricity he had promised. He was far from the first to recognise this defect. The Town Council of Tel Aviv, by mid 1921, already ahead of the game, had recognised that the flow would be insufficient for the electricity they needed. Even then they had been exploring the possibility of using diesel generators and had sought German expertise. And Rutenberg, who had been in discussions with the Tel Aviv Council, had been aware of the problem well before his concession had been granted. It was their arguments about the impracticality of a hydro-electric plan that eventually persuaded him to change course. Using the excuse that the price being charged for land by the Arabs was prohibitive, he began to explore the diesel option. It was then that he discovered that the cost of British machinery was much higher than that which he could buy from Germany. Now there were two issues with which he had to contend. How to convince the Government firstly to allow him to change from hydro- to diesel-powered generation, and secondly, to agree to him buying his machinery from the recently defeated enemy, Germany.

How he managed to deal with both of these, despite opposition from his own legal advisors and despite personal rebukes in Parliament, provides a lesson in negotiating skills and is testament to his powers of persuasion.

Rutenberg seemed saddled with the hydro-electric scheme. Diesel was the only solution, but how to get that past the Administration? His brother Abraham and his lawyer Harry Sacher were concerned about the political and legal implications of what he was proposing (*Fig. 24*). He would lose out if the Government saw his failure as a reason to stop the whole process and the Arabs would see it as a successful result on their part. Rutenberg could not abide the prospect of going through the whole tedious negotiating process yet again and decided to press ahead regardless. At the end of 1921 he decided to negotiate with the Government in London. He explained to Colonial Office officials that the Arabs were proving difficult about his hydro-electric plans. They were seeking far too much money for the land he needed next to the river. He would be able to persuade them to sell to him given enough time but

Figure 24: Abraham Rutenberg, Pinchas's younger brother and partner in his Electricity Company

meanwhile there was an immediate need to supply electricity. In a stroke of impudence he tentatively offered a solution, albeit temporary, to what he presented as the Government's problem. If he might be allowed, he would help by installing a diesel-powered generator for the time being. He was not getting rid of the river scheme, simply delaying it. Here Rutenberg demonstrated his technique of dissimulation. He knew full well that a hydro-system was never going to work, yet he didn't even hint that it was now completely off the agenda. He could provide the diesel plant by August 1923, ahead of the September deadline, while giving the impression that, if granted an extension of the time, the hydro-electric scheme would follow after more negotiation with the Arab landowners. The High Commissioner, pleased to have some sort of resolution to the problem, gained Colonial Office approval within a few days providing it did not set any precedent for his major Jordan River scheme.

Officials in the Colonial Office, confused and only partially aware of the background, agreed to a delay the Auja River scheme.

There was something Machiavellian about his behaviour during this time. The power generating plant he now proposed was sited well to the south between Jaffa and Tel Aviv, near to where he had intended to place a distribution centre but nowhere near the original position by the river. It was built at what is now HaHashmal Street, Hashmal is Hebrew for electricity (*Fig. 2, page 16*). When the time eventually came to consider re-instating the hydro-electric scheme, the plan was repeatedly delayed then quietly dropped.

The problem of where to purchase the diesel equipment was next. He had all the information about costs to hand. As early as three months before the concession was granted, he had discovered the difference in prices between British and German manufacturers and knew that it would cause difficulties. Should he support the Empire and go for British equipment as the Government expected? Or should he seek the best deal he could get for his Company and its shareholders? This was before he had obtained funds from the TFA from which he had agreed to purchase only from British firms. He sought the advice of Weizmann who confirmed that he should go for the most economically viable deal. He had already agreed with the Colonial Office that he would buy British if their charges were no more than 10% higher than elsewhere. But now he was faced with estimates from British firms that were at least twice the price of the same equipment from German companies. The price sought by British companies for turbines, transformers and alternators was £25,878 compared with £14,224 by German firms. Even transportation was more expensive; from Britain it was three times what it would cost from Germany. It was only copper wire, that cost some 8% more from a British company, that fell within the 10% limit that the company could bear, and the wire was bought from Britain.

As he was on the way to Germany at the end of the year, he wrote a letter directly to Winston Churchill in tones that suggested a more intimate relationship than he actually had. 'May I at the outset apologise for encroaching on your valuable time, but the urgency of the following matters makes it imperative that I should address you with as little delay as possible.' An arrogant attempt to get an instant response to an issue on which Rutenberg had been cogitating for some months. He continued, 'I collected data regarding the cost of the machinery and materials required for my project. I found that the lowest English tender was 98% in excess of tenders made in Germany. The purchase in England … would accordingly involve an additional expenditure of several hundreds of thousands of pounds, and thus increase the rates of energy, rates of transport and cost of living in Palestine and so retard the economic development of the country.' There it was; the whole future of the Palestine Mandate was at risk unless he could buy his equipment in Germany. He goes on to explain his dilemma, 'The placing of orders in Germany, however, might lead to undesirable political consequences in this country.' Hardly an understatement. Sir Herbert Samuel, he wrote, had accepted the need to purchase in the cheapest market but now he, Rutenberg, needed to speak personally to Churchill to gain his views. Then he used the argument that 'The Arab-Jewish difficulties can be readily solved by their participation in practical and reproductive work in this country. I intend to spend the Christmas holidays in making a personal study in Germany of the questions to which I have referred, but before I go, I consider it of the first importance that I should have your opinions and observations in the matter.' Then the last piece of 'Chutzpah', 'In view of the fact that I propose to leave for Germany tomorrow evening, you will appreciate my desiring such an interview as soon as possible.'

It is unclear whether Churchill met Pinchas as he passed through London, but he did not raise objections to his proposals.

It is entirely possible that Rutenberg did not believe he could gain a meeting but simply needed to get the issue on record at the highest level. Certainly, the idea that he might buy his kit from the recent enemy was not without considerable political fallout but officials in London held their noses and granted him permission to go ahead with the cheaper, German, purchase. Naturally it was picked up in the press and in Parliament but the opprobrium to which he was subject did not deter him as he and Meir Dizengoff, the Mayor of Tel Aviv, reached Berlin. There they rapidly agreed a deal and by January 1922 the first orders were placed for two 500 horsepower diesel engines from the manufacturer Voith. Foreign Office officials only became fully aware of the details of the deal in July while the British manufacturers, Vickers and the English Electric Company, were incensed. The only British purchase was for copper wire.

One of the biggest manufacturers in Europe was AEG and their engineers were heavily involved with Rutenberg in the design and choice of equipment. There were six AEG consultants based in Tel Aviv helping with the installation, and Rutenberg's Jaffa Electric Company opened an office in Berlin. He clearly meant business and Germany was in a lead position.

The diesel generator began operation in June 1923 and, as we have seen, started providing the power for lighting along Allenby Street in Tel Aviv. Electric lighting had only been installed in the House of Commons, in 1912, and now, some eleven years later, it was the turn of Palestine. Recognising the sensitivities in London and the opposition amongst the Arabs, he had wanted celebrations to be muted to avoid even more provocation. But in that at least he failed.

The negotiations with the Jaffa city leadership were tortuous and prolonged. Despite having gained a loan of £25,000 for the city, Rutenberg found himself in a series of disputes and legal cases about obscure details of where electricity cables may be sited, where poles may be placed on pavements and reimbursement for plans not adhered to. Some Arabs were vocal in their opposition to any deals with Rutenberg while others were demanding that they should be connected to the supply and share in the benefits electricity would bestow. Rutenberg tried his best. He made sure his staff learnt Arabic and pressed them to go out of their way to be helpful to Arab householders. It took some years for these problems to be sorted out but finally Jaffa as well as Tel Aviv became increasingly electrified.

By 1925, when the Jaffa powerhouse (no longer named the Auja River Project) was fully operational, Rutenberg's company began the purchase of replacement transformers from Britain as he was now obliged to do by his agreement with the Trade Facilities Agency. A 1,125 horsepower engine was ordered from Fraser and Chalmers and began producing electricity in 1926, and Rutenberg was opening two more diesel plants, in Haifa and Tiberius. Some years later he set up another power station, this time north of Tel Aviv, that became known as 'Reading Power Station' named after Lord Reading, the first Chairman of Rutenberg's Palestine Electric Company (*Fig 25*).

There were yet more obstacles to be overcome. The rules and regulations surrounding the supply of electricity in the UK were detailed and complicated. It was when an effort was made to apply the same Ordinance Legislation to Palestine that Rutenberg objected. On receiving the 62 pages of draft regulations, he commented that the numerous penalties would keep the Law Courts busy but did not do anything to help supply electricity. The laws may have been suitable for Western industrialised conurbations, but they were completely inappropriate for a Palestine with little in the way of industry. He argued for more than two years before a compromise was finally agreed.

He had tried to get the concession from the Government to supply electricity for the manufacture of railway engines in Haifa but the owners were suspicious about his ability to deliver. They preferred to develop their own electricity generators but, regardless of opposition, he pressed ahead with his own plans. The diesel power plant in Haifa was built within

Figure 25: Reading Power Station as it is today

12 months and was operational by 1924. He soon had more customers than he needed to make it a commercial success. He renamed his company from The Jaffa to The Palestine Electric Company, with Lord Reading as its chairman. By 1928 his company was producing electricity for much of Palestine. In 1926 it produced over three million kWh for six thousand customers and by 1929, almost five million kWh for over nine thousand customers. He was able to report an unexpected profit of £6,000 by the end of 1925 and dividends were payable to the shareholders.

By now industrialisation had progressed so much that he no longer felt it necessary for an electrified railway to take up spare capacity. Manufacture of building materials, print, textiles, food, chemicals and food were booming, and he had secured a Government contract from the Air Ministry High Command. There were many stipulations about the security of supply to such a sensitive Government military establishment. He had no compunction in jumping through the hoops despite the loss it incurred. He soon made up for the deficit when he took the opportunity of using the supply lines needed, to branch out and provide electricity to a number of towns and villages en route to the Air Ministry buildings.

Production rates rose so much that some began to wonder whether the hydro-electric generator on the Jordan River was really needed. Views were being expressed in the Colonial Office and amongst the Zionists, that there was no need for it. Weizmann too, was sceptical about the need for this type of generator when diesel powered generators were doing so well. But all that ignored the rather more important bonuses that came from building the plant on the Jordan as we will see.

The purchase of machinery only from Britain had by now become an obligation. He had entered into it with the UK Trade Facilities Agency in order to gain their approval for a large grant. Much to the annoyance of potential American funders, he no longer needed their support and his company was sufficiently established to be able to cope with the high price of British goods.

How Rutenberg managed to gain approval for his plans and to put them into action is one of the more fascinating stories of the early Mandate period. It was a mixture of audacity, logical argument, working behind closed doors in secret, persuasive determination and an eye kept firmly on his ultimate aim. He was not deterred by a need to change his plans when it became obvious that his initial ideas were no longer valid. And he played his cards not only close to his chest but very carefully as he dissembled, when required, to gain his way with the Government. If he was overbearing, pugnacious and argumentative he also showed himself to be a brilliant negotiator. He must have seemed agreeable and sufficiently flexible to have convinced others to go along with his ideas. A very clever man, a hard one with whom to deal but ultimately a successful one.

CHAPTER 15

Naharayim; the 'Two Rivers' project

We must now return to the Jordan River power plant and the negotiations with the French and British Governments about the sources of the River Jordan. Rutenberg, as always, was heavily involved, although on this occasion with less success.

The report he presented to Samuel in July 1920 envisaged the waters of the Litani and Yarmouk Rivers being available to supplement the flow in the Jordan. Without them the rate of flow in the Jordan would be barely sufficient to generate the electricity he needed, or so he said. The problem was that those rivers arose outside the Palestinian frontiers then under discussion. The Litani passed east to west across Lebanon well to the north of the border that was being hotly debated and, in any event, would have had to be channelled across land to reach the Jordan, while the Yarmouk arose in Trans-Jordan (*Diagram 1, page 78*).

For the moment it seemed that the agricultural and industrial development of Palestine was entirely dependent on the water available, not only for Rutenberg's critical electrification plan but also for the irrigation of a water-starved Palestine. Britain's Foreign Office was pressing hard and on the same side as Rutenberg for once. Little wonder that negotiations between France and Britain on where the border between their Mandatories was to be placed had reached such a difficult stage. But less wonder that Rutenberg became involved.

Discussions on borders had started between Lloyd George and Clemenceau even before the 1919 Peace Conference, continuing at the Conference and thereafter at San Remo in 1920. It was only resolved in 1924. Britain argued that the border should be on the Litani River but the French would not hear of it. They stuck firmly to their belief that the border outlined in the much earlier Sykes-Picot agreement, should be the one adopted, even though that agreement had been overtaken by events. The negotiations became more fractious as Alexandre Millerand took over from the more amenable Clemenceau as President of France. Millerand was not the least sympathetic to the British plan to develop Palestine and even less supportive of the Zionists. He only reluctantly, and with bad grace, agreed that the wording of the Balfour Declaration could be included in the San Remo report. Pouring over maps provided enough problems in trying to identify other borders, especially the one on the east that extended north and south from the biblical 'Dan to Beersheba' and it was agreed to leave the difficult decision on the whereabouts of Palestine's northern border to a later date. The key British figures in the prolonged negotiations that followed were Robert Vansittart based in Paris and Eric Forbes Adam in the Foreign Office in London. Vansittart's advice was influential, and as Private Secretary to Foreign Secretary Lord Curzon carried significant weight. He recognised that the French were very firm on their definition of the border and unlikely to be moved, and he recommended that Britain should press hard for an agreement as soon as possible in order to repair relations with the French that were becoming increasingly fraught. He now asked whether Britain should risk arguing with the French simply to please the Zionists? He clearly thought they should not.

Weizmann too was urging more caution and he was not the only one; the Foreign Secretary himself also hoped that by stringing it out they might reach a better understanding. Weizmann even persuaded Louis Brandeis in America to write to Lloyd George urging greater pressure on the French.

It was now that Rutenberg sprang into action. Frustrated that his electrification scheme was under threat he started banging his drum. He made the siting of the border an absolutely essential factor in the future of electrification and hence of the successful development of the country. In London in August 1920, he confronted Forbes-Adam with his demands for more action against the French. By October he was in Paris but not before a battle for a visa that was refused. Again, he marshalled his arguments. He reminded the French authorities how helpful he had been to them when he was in Odessa in 1918. He told them to forget rumours that he was a Bolshevik when in fact he had worked with the 'White Russians' against the Bolsheviks and helped the French in their escape from the Red Army. He did not fail to point out that he also saved them money when he exposed certain senior military officers who had been purloining funds. His sole interest was now in an electrification scheme that was vital for the future of Palestine.

His plea worked and he gained his visa. More impressive is the fact that he was granted an audience with Millerand to present his case. Unfortunately for him, his blunt methods failed to work on the French President. Vansittart too was startled by Rutenberg's forthright approach and thought that it was bound to be counterproductive for his and the Zionists' case. Outright aggression was unlikely to work in the more subtle world in which he and French diplomats dwelled.

It was now clear that the bid for Litani River waters was going to fail and Vansittart recommended that, given a little more time and when cooler heads prevailed, an attempt should be made to gain more from the Yarmouk River in Trans-Jordan and from the eastern edge of Lake Kineret that lay outside British-controlled territory. Eventually a quiet agreement along those lines was reached informally in December 1920, and Rutenberg was able to move ahead without the waters of the Litani. It was obvious by now that not everyone succumbed to his school of charm.

It is notable however that the fact that he was able to go to the very top of the French Government to present his views showed him to be someone to whom attention was being paid. He was increasingly regarded in London as not only an expert but as an activist who did not mind whom he upset to get his way. His enthusiasm and know-how were widely respected, but many began to fear him and his methods. These characteristics, of a man who could get things done, stood him in good stead when an international committee was set up with expert representatives from France and Britain to consider the needs of Palestine for water in the north. The need for technical collaboration inevitably led to Rutenberg being invited to join the committee. Naturally, he dominated the discussions as someone who knew more than most about what was required. The outcome was that he emerged as a significant power-broker in the development of policy for Palestine.

And, as we will see, he did gain at least some of the water flow he needed to generate his electricity. It was soon shown to be enough.

CHAPTER 16

More hurdles

During the next few years he was distracted by a call to take on a more politically overt role. His appeal was obvious. His reputation as a man of action had spread. His revolutionary background appealed to Jewish socialists and his commercial credentials were admired by the right wing. He was an obvious choice for leadership and the 'Yishuv', the Jewish population, elected him to the chair of their representative body, the Va'ad HaLeumi. He was never going to be an ideal politician nor was he entirely comfortable in the role. He soon found himself in difficulties, as we will find in Chapter 19, but when he resigned he was pleased to find himself free to concentrate on his first love, busy action on the ground. The hydro-electric generator on the Jordan River consumed much of his passion and energy for the next few years.

But they were not easy years in the world at large and certainly not in Palestine.

The international background against which he was operating was far from encouraging. American and European economies were sorely stretched. Unemployment in Britain and the USA was running high, the great depression, culminating in the American 'Crash' of 1929, and the strikes in Britain were distracting attention from Rutenberg's quest for funds.

In Palestine things were even worse. Cattle plagues in 1926, earthquakes in 1927 that saw many rendered homeless or dead, and droughts and plagues of locusts in 1928 and 1929 were scarcely welcoming to immigrants. The economy was in severe straits, unemployment amongst the Jews reached 6,000 in 1926 and, in 1927 for the first time, the number of Jews leaving Palestine exceeded the number entering. And to cap it all, the Palestinian Arab Congress in 1928 again voiced its determined opposition to Balfour.

These were the circumstances under which Rutenberg was struggling. It was in March 1926 that he was finally given the Government's concession to move ahead with his plans on the Jordan River and he had gathered the finance to begin.

Inevitably, there had been a series of problems with British officialdom conspiring to delay his programme. There was a strong sense that Colonial Office officials were seeking ways to hold back permission. They procrastinated by seeking clarifications and detailed explanations dragging on for years. They were certainly in no hurry despite the fact that Britain would have gained the benefits of electrification to build up the harbour in Haifa and accelerate the development of the oil pipeline from Iraq, as well as the airport at Lydda. Rutenberg's level of frustration was growing as the delay stretched to five years.

He was pressing hard to gain permission to provide electricity to Trans-Jordan as well as Palestine and knew that it had been included in his original concession. High Commissioner Field Marshal Plumer was of a different opinion. He believed, not without reason, that the Arabs in Palestine and in Jordan would resist any idea of extending the reach of electrification. The Colonial Office were similarly opposed but had difficulty handling the legal consequences of reneging on a concession already agreed. Rutenberg tried hard to help. He offered to provide, free of charge, all the infrastructure and building for two plants, at Amman and As Salt in Trans-Jordan. His aim was to retain technical control of electricity generation, but the fear for the Arabs was that he would see it as opening the prospect of the sale of land for Jewish immigration east of the Jordan River. It was indeed Rutenberg's long-term aim and he was to make further attempts later.

While there were many amongst the Bedouin in Trans-Jordan who were happy to sell their land, Plumer was very sensitive to the opinion amongst Arabs more generally. His successor, Sir John Chancellor, was even more inclined to support Arab claims, especially in 1929, the year of serious riots against the Jews. The uprising was ostensibly because of a religious dispute at the Western Wall in Jerusalem but, in reality, it was a reflection of Arab resistance to land purchase and immigration by the Jews. Any effort to extend the area of land for Jews to occupy, east of the Jordan River, was never going to be tolerated without further blood-shed. The High Commissioner would only agree to Rutenberg gaining access to Trans-Jordan if he could persuade the Emir Abdullah to accept his blandishments. A further attempt was made much later when Rutenberg and Abdullah had friendly discussions but the Emir, fearful of reprisals, withdrew yet again. Rutenberg never did supply electricity beyond Palestine to the East of the Jordan, but this prolonged period of uncertainty added to the delay and to his frustration. It was the High Commissioner who was left to put a block on Rutenberg's plans for Trans-Jordan. While Rutenberg was well aware that he had had the legal concession to Trans-Jordan before Churchill had come along and split that country off, he decided not to press the case. He banked it as a measure of good-will that he could use in later negotiations.

Then there was the problem, unforeseen in the Colonial Office, inherent in constructing a power plant that required a base on both sides of the Jordan River. It seems to have come as a surprise that such a huge undertaking would require access for building on both sides of the river. The Colonial Office was in no position to consider altering the border so painfully resolved only recently, to find a strip of land on the eastern side of the river. A trip to London in March 1925, saw Rutenberg negotiating with the then Colonial Secretary, Leo Amery, who agreed to everything except extending the concession to supply electricity to Trans-Jordan. Rutenberg, knowing he would not get further on this issue, accepted the stricture as a way to move forward. As usual, he retreated with the idea firmly in mind that he would return to it in the fullness of time. High Commissioner Plumer then agreed to release the land and river waters he needed from the eastern bank of the river.

Rutenberg was champing at the bit, and a year later, in March 1926, he was belatedly able to start work.

By 1931, having retreated from the political battlefield in which he was badly bruised, he was back supervising his beloved hydro-electric plant on the Jordan.

Then disaster struck. A huge downpour overwhelmed a dam half built and flooded the power plant. Several transformers were ruined, one of his men was badly injured and the scheme was put back by several months. He was concerned that shareholders might withdraw their support and raising more money was problematic. Lord Reading, Chairman of his Board, was increasingly worried but Rutenberg was used by now to shrugging off setbacks and on he ploughed.

His mastery of detail and ability to manage such a complicated project, and put it into action against reluctant officialdom speaks for someone with unusual capacity and skills. A brief outline can give only a hint of the complexity of the practical building programme (*Diagrams 4 and 5*).

His huge power plant became known as Naharayim (Two Rivers) as it was sited at the junction of the rivers Jordan and Yarmouk. It required a complex series of dams, reservoirs

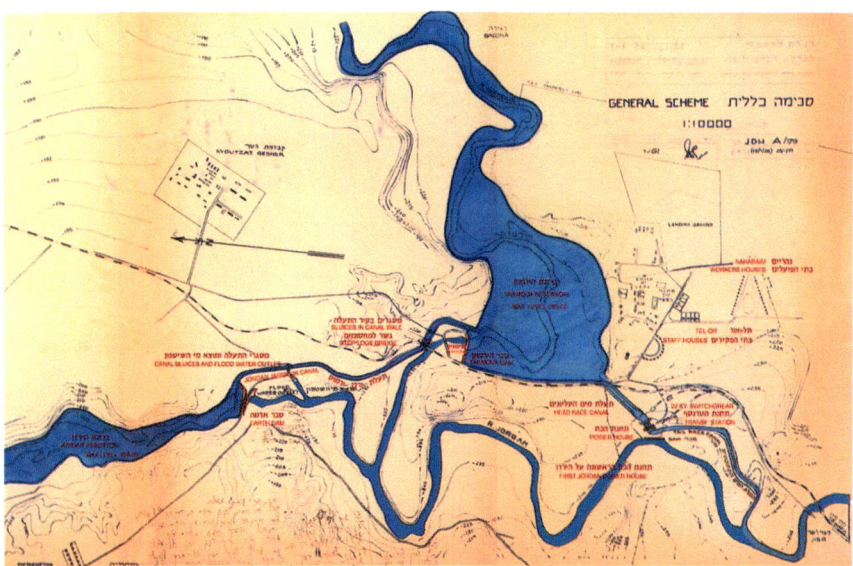

Diagram 4: Rutenberg's dams and canals at Naharayim (original diagram)

and canals, the diversion of the Damascus rail link and the construction of roads and a bridge across the Jordan. Lake Tiberius was enlarged and a new reservoir covering 7,000 square metres was created on the Yarmouk River.

High-tension cables to Haifa and Tel Aviv were laid and it was all elaborated in a very full article in *The Times* of February 25th 1929 headed, 'Harnessing the Jordan; Electric Power for Palestine.' 'The Jordan Power-House will consist of three 8,000 horsepower turbine generator units, and of a fourth later, when definite data on the amount of water available has been obtained. A second power-plant is to be created at Abadich when the demand for power rises …' At this stage there were no limits to Rutenberg's ambitions. 'If necessary, a third power-house will be built to the North of Lake Tiberius.' *The Times* correspondent goes on to describe the ease with which Rutenberg's workers were able to move across the river into Jordan without creating problems at the border. He was taken by the enthusiasm of the workforce and by the way they were treated. The two thousand workers employed in the scheme were housed locally in the simple

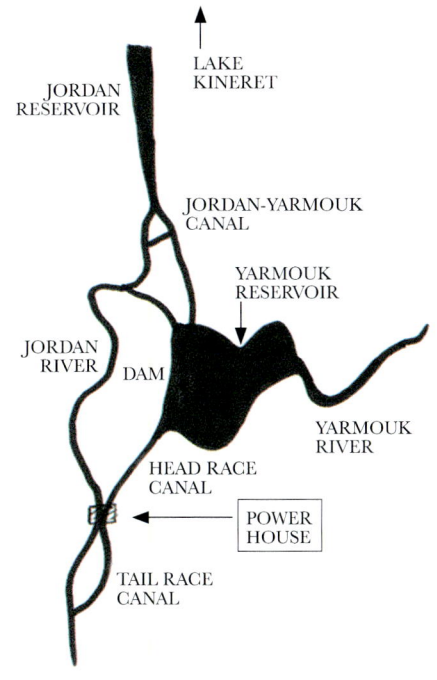

Diagram 5: Simplified diagram of arrangements around the Power House on the Jordan

accommodation available. 'What has always been a plague spot is now a place where men enjoy real health and happiness; scientific and sensible feeding has done this and unremitting attention to details – such as waking up a man in the middle of the night if he forgets or neglects his mosquito net.' Despite the high incidence of malaria in nearby Arab villages it was less than 2% in the workers' camps. Food was provided below cost, 'No man is allowed to miss a meal in order to save a few piastres'. In a note of wonder he describes how, 'The canteen is entirely non-alcoholic – not because there is a prohibition of intoxicating liquor, but because there is no demand for it'.

By 1929, when the newspaper article appeared, it was clear that the anti-Zionist and anti-Rutenberg rhetoric of *The Times* had long disappeared.

It is notable that all his workers were immigrant Jews. Mostly from Poland, they were industrious and highly intelligent, talking politics and philosophy late into the night.

Rutenberg made sure that his workers felt the majesty of their work in a paper in Russian he circulated amongst them. 'This project is an important source of existence for our people… Keep this in mind at all times. Each one of you should be worthy of the great honour of being part of this. We need not only the strength of your muscles, but also your souls and the greatest endeavour of each and every one of you. I am sure you will give of your best.'

'Arise!'

A very Lenin-style inspirational message.

The Times reporter was almost certainly unaware of the very strong grip that Rutenberg kept on his workers. Prohibited from joining a union they were completely dependent on him for their pay and care. He treated them well, but only if they relied exclusively on him for their working conditions. While he thought that he was a benign father figure to his workers, they may well have felt otherwise at times. This paternalism brought him into conflict with the Histradut, the Trade Union movement, but they, wisely, decided not to pursue it too far. They knew that Rutenberg employed such a large proportion of the total work force they would only lose out especially at a time of high unemployment.

Rutenberg had already recognised that his workers would need protection in the event of an Arab uprising and had asked for support. None was forthcoming from the High Commissioner and he simply mobilised his own defence force from amongst his workers who took their turns on night watch.

At a time of increasing discontent and faltering employment amongst the Jews, he was able to offer employment that raised morale and that in turn encouraged immigration.

Building the power-house was a massive undertaking; it took until 9th of June 1932 before electricity began to flow.

The opening ceremony was held in the presence of High Commissioner Sir Arthur Grenfell Wauchope, (the fifth High Commissioner that Rutenberg had seen come and go since Herbert Samuel), the Emir Abdullah of Jordan, Colonel Cox, British Governor of the Emirate of Jordan, and many other dignitaries (*Fig. 26*).

The Times, on June 10th, 1932, under the heading 'Hydro-Electric Power in Palestine. Jordan Station Opened.' was laudatory.

Quoting the High Commissioner 'His Excellency, in a highly complimentary speech, congratulated M. Rutenberg on the accomplishment of what could not have been achieved in Palestine except for his gifts of leadership, enthusiasm, and doggedness in overcoming obstacles. The plant can now provide 12,000,000 units a year and will ultimately supply 65,000,000 to the Palestine Electric Corporation, formed under stations at Jaffa, Haifa and Tiberias.'

It was a significant moment for Rutenberg of course but by then the economy had begun to grow, with large numbers of customers for his electricity. In 1929, before his plant on the river opened, he was supplying 3.6 million KWHours of

Figure 26: Naharayim, the Two Rivers Power Plant on the Jordan River

electricity to about nine thousand customers. By 1933 he was selling over 20 million KWHours to 22,000 customers (*Fig. 27*).

All this during a period of serious Arab unrest.

He tried again to engage the Emir of Jordan in a supply of licence-free electricity but despite some interest it fell by the wayside in the face of Palestinian Arab threats. They had been mobilising their opposition to Jewish immigration and, under Haj Amin Husseini, had been writing to the League of Nations to seek their support to abandon the Mandate and the Zionists' quest, including Rutenberg's plans.

Rutenberg had managed against the odds to see his electrification plans come to fruition. He had built up a considerable reputation by now as a man who got things done at a time when the obstacles to Zionism had seemed

Figure 27: Naharayim

Figure 28: Naharayim Power Plant destroyed by Jordan during the 1948 War of Independence

Figure 29: Solar panels floating on a reservoir at the site of the Naharayim reservoir on the Yarmouk River. Israel's new form of electricity generator

insurmountable. Certainly an entrepreneur, but also acutely aware of the need to provide his own brand of support for his workers and the working population. His commitment to socialism was undiminished despite his obvious commercial success. But it was his own brand of socialism that he fostered, not one that included much in the way of democratic inclusivity. And his acute dislike of politicians and leading international Zionists was undiminished. His Naharayim plant continued to produce electricity until 1948 when, in the war of independence, it was destroyed by the Jordanians. It was never to be rebuilt (*Fig. 28*). There is now a huge solar panel generating system at the site. To keep it cool it floats on a reservoir at the site of Rutenberg's original Yarmouk river reservoir, testament to Israeli ingenuity (*Fig. 29*).

For some time there had been discussion both in London and Jerusalem about whether there really was a need for hydro-electricity in Palestine. There was the suspicion too amongst the Zionists and within the Colonial Office that the whole scheme was a straight commercial enterprise to provide profits for its shareholders rather than a national asset for the Jewish people. Weizmann was particularly critical. In a speech in Jerusalem in 1935 he said that if he had known how much the hydro-electric scheme was designed for profit and not for the Jewish homeland, he would have opposed it. In vain did Rutenberg try to portray the Electric Company as an important instrument of the Hebrew people.

The value of hydro-electric generation was undermined by its reliance on an unpredictable supply of water, its expense, and the fact that diesel power generation was simpler and cheaper. It was not long before it was overtaken by diesel. It is significant that neither in Palestine nor modern-day Israel has anyone seen fit to build a new hydro-electric power-house. But does it suggest that Rutenberg was wrong in his contention that his hydro-electric scheme was essential for the future development of the Jewish homeland?

Many reasons can be adduced as to its value.

Firstly, its symbolic significance cannot be ignored. It gave a sense of an important aim and achievement to the Jews of Palestine. Something they could unite in supporting. Secondly, it demonstrated to the British Government that, at little cost to itself, agricultural and industrial development could be promoted in a part of the world sadly lacking such signs of advancement. Thirdly, it offered employment to hundreds of workers at a time when unemployment was running high. Fourthly, it highlighted the need for investment in road building, transport and other infrastructure projects. And all this activity provided a boost to immigration when diaspora Jews were uncertain about the attractiveness of a country where life was far from easy.

It boosted morale enormously and nowhere was this more obvious than amongst Rutenberg's workers. He knew how to galvanise them with his 'Arise!' And it encouraged considerable foreign investment.

For these reasons its value went well beyond its utilitarian function.

There is no doubt, however, that the 'Old Man of Naharayim'

did very well for himself. His income of £8,000 per annum raised eyebrows. In contrast, the average income of a senior official in the Jewish agency was £240 per annum. By 1935 the Electric Company was floated on the London stock market. Rutenberg's share of the proceeds saw him gain £20,000 plus 50,000 shares for the transfer of the concession. He was a wealthy man when he built his own mansion in characteristic heavy Imperial style on Mount Carmel in Haifa. And living alone he did not lack support staff who tended to his needs. Nor, apparently, did he lack female company according to reports of nocturnal visitors. We should draw a veil over a possible affair with a woman married to one of his senior employees. Details are lacking and since his own marriage had long since been broken it is not surprising that he may have indulged.

A picture of surprisingly warm domesticity was drawn in her diary by Blanche Dugdale, affectionately known as 'Daffy'. She was the niece of Arthur Balfour, about whom she had written a biography, a friend of Chaim Weizmann and a strong Zionist. She befriended Rutenberg whom she referred to as Peter. She visited him at his home in April 1939 and stayed for the Passover Seder night celebrations. These commemorate the Jewish exodus from Egypt and are a time devoted to children and family. Pinchas showed her over his 'beautiful house; high spacious rooms looking out on all sides, and one of the most beautiful views in this world… Dear Peter, a real creator. This is the first real family Seder at which I have been.' Then comes the surprise revelation about the involvement of children in the ceremony. 'Little David asked the Questions – Sandy opened the door for Elijah – here on the Carmel! What a wonderful experience to be at one with these people.' There is no indication that Pinchas had any young children at this stage of his life and it seems highly likely that they were his brother Abraham's grandchildren.

When he died in 1942, he left all his possessions in an endowment fund for Jewish education. The total value was some £160,000 of which the majority was made up of shares in the Palestine Electric Company and his house valued at £12,000. His home now houses the Rutenberg Institute at 77 Hanassi Avenue in Haifa where courses and seminars are run for students from around the world.

But back in the 1930s he was to become involved in more overtly political activities and it soon became clear that he had been a much more successful businessman and entrepreneur than the politician he was persuaded to become.

First, however, we must deal with the strange case of Euripides Mavromatis.

CHAPTER 17

The Mavromatis disraction

Euripides Mavromatis, a Greek with Turkish citizenship, had gained a franchise from the Ottomans to provide electricity for Jerusalem in 1914 while Palestine was still a Turkish possession. It seemed to Herbert Samuel that, since the Ottomans had been defeated, all agreements with them were null and void by 1920. But it was not so simple and when Mavromatis learnt that Rutenberg had been granted the concession for electricity generation in September 1921 he sprang into action. He demanded that his concession should take precedence over that of Rutenberg which he said was illegal since it had been granted before Britain had signed a Treaty with Turkey, (that was not signed until 1923 at Lausanne) and before the Mandate had been ratified by the League of Nations (that was not confirmed until August 1923). If he was not awarded the franchise now, he would seek compensation to the sum of £234,339. Needless to say, the compensation he sought was regarded as outrageous and his bid was summarily rejected by the British.

He did not stop there and pressed his case in the media in England, and with Members of Parliament at a time when there was already opposition to Rutenberg and his plans. When he got little further, he took to the law and his representatives began a correspondence with the Colonial Office in London. They too were politely turned back. It was then, in 1924, that matters took a much more serious turn for Britain when Mavromatis's lawyers persuaded the Greek Government to take up the case on his behalf. Having had a short exchange of letters with the Colonial Office, they decided to try their luck at the Permanent Court of International Justice in Geneva. Much to the UK Government's surprise and irritation it became an expensive and very distracting episode at a time when they least needed it. Although, by the time the case was heard Mavromatis had removed his claim on the Jordan River and concentrated on the Jaffa and Jerusalem concessions, it was still more than an irritation for the British Government.

A reading of the lengthy Judgement published on the 30th of August is not to be recommended for the busy reader, or even for those with plenty of time, especially if they are not steeped in the law. But here I will attempt to summarise. Most of the legal debate was taken up by a discussion about whether the Court was entitled to take a judgement on the case before it. 'Of course it is', said His Excellency M Politis for the Greeks. While the Court has been set up to examine disputes between League of Nations Countries and not between individual citizens and States, Greece was entitled to appeal on behalf of one of its citizens where it believes he is being treated illegally by the actions of another State. Secondly, all avenues for a satisfactorily negotiated resolution had been pursued without success and recourse to the Court was now necessary. Thirdly, it was the British Government that had issued the concession to an official authority in its Mandatory and it was therefore the Government that was responsible for an illegal act before a Treaty with Turkey had been signed and before the League of Nations had granted the Mandate. A tortuous debate followed on whether these were adequate reasons for the Court to be able to take a view.

Was Greece entitled to bring the case for Mavromatis? Had there been enough effort made to resolve the disagreement before bringing the case to the Court? Had the British Government acted illegally in granting its concession? And was it the officially designated Authority in Palestine or the Zionist Organization that was granted the concession or was it an individual, Pinchas Rutenberg? On the latter point Chaim Weizmann was pressed into action as leader of the Z.O. He and Rutenberg were at pains to point out that while the Z.O. were supportive, it was to Rutenberg himself that the concession was granted. After much dancing on the heads of pins the court decided; Para 22, 'Once a State has taken up a case on behalf of one of its subjects before an international tribunal, in the eyes of the latter the State is the sole claimant. The fact that Great Britain and Greece are the opposing Parties to the dispute arising out of the Mavromatis concessions is sufficient to make it a dispute between two States within the meaning of Article 26 of the Palestine Mandate.' They went on to accept that sufficient effort had been made to settle the dispute by negotiation before approaching the Court. They did so by accepting the doubtful argument that negotiations undertaken by Mavromatis himself, before the Greek Government took over his case, could be counted towards the much less extensive negotiations that they themselves undertook later. They then agreed that the franchise awarded to Mavromatis for the Jerusalem electrification scheme was reasonable and acceptable.

However, the Court also accepted that the concession to Rutenberg had been made to him as a private contractor and was, therefore, as valid as that which had been made to Mavromatis before the War.

On this basis they agreed that it would be unreasonable for Mavromatis's claim on the Jaffa plant to take precedence over Rutenberg's plan. Thus, only Mavromatis's Jerusalem bid was approved. 'The Court therefore, having ascertained that it only has jurisdiction to entertain the claim relating to Jerusalem, reserves this claim for judgment on its merits and declares that its jurisdiction does not extend to the claim relating to the works at Jaffa.'

They also dismissed the Greek Government claim for expenses and a further, similar bid by Mavromatis was rejected, by which time it was 1927. Despite the rejection, Britain was left with a large legal bill.

Of course, there was far from complete consensus amongst the Judges. No less than five of the twelve provided dissenting submissions at some length. They suggested that the Court should not be in the position of taking on the type of case with which they were now dealing. But the majority decision was agreed. There is more than a hint of similar shaky foundations for the legitimacy of the Court to judge the case brought by the Palestinian Authority in 2019 against Israel for alleged war crimes. At least in the case of Greece versus Britain it was one between recognised Nation States. In the end Mavromatis was left with his concession to provide electricity for a tram system, lighting and irrigation in Jerusalem. He then turned down an offer of £80,000 from Rutenberg as being far too small.

Rutenberg was disappointed but far from devastated. He made light of the decision at an interview to journalists when he pointed out that constructing an electrification plant for Jerusalem would be difficult and unprofitable for many years. The population was poor and the demand for electricity was low. The land was rocky and mountainous and the drilling for water channels would be hazardous. In other words, he gave the impression that he was pleased to be out of any obligations for this city. He was left with supplying electricity for the whole of Palestine apart from Jerusalem and within a 20 kilometre radius from the Church of the Holy Sepulchre in the Old City.

Having been given the franchise by the Mandatory Government, Mavromatis now sold it on, in 1928, to Balfour-Beatty, a British company, that went on to establish the Jerusalem Electric and Public Service Corporation. It soon encountered the problems predicted by Rutenberg, staggering on during the 1930s and 40s trying to supply enough electricity for Jerusalem. Later, the Mandate sought the help of the Palestine Electric Company to provide the current. Rutenberg was no longer alive when this final nail was hammered into the Mavromatis venture.

CHAPTER 18

Origins of a politician

We can now turn to Rutenberg's second career, as a politician. It was less successful despite an enormous amount of effort. His character did not suit democratic governance and the art of the possible entailing political concessions. It was thrust upon him in 1929 by a population deeply divided and unhappy with their then leadership. He was certainly a leader of men, but not one who brooked argument nor one who listened to opposition.

He had achieved his first objective by 1922, the diesel-powered generator near to Jaffa and his hydro-electric plant on the Jordan River was to start operation in 1932. But now he was distracted by calls to take on a more overtly political role.

It is little wonder that by 1929 he was something of a national hero to the Jews of Palestine. He was the man who, seemingly single-handedly, had explored the land, drawn up detailed plans for an electrification scheme on which the whole future of the promised land had apparently depended, had overcome prolonged opposition from the Government and the Arabs, had convinced those with the money to release it for his scheme and was now demonstrating the end results in the physical manifestation of massive and successful power plants. And he was a large-scale employer, supportive of his workers and giving them security and reasonable pay. The Jews wondered what more could this 'heroic' figure do for them?

Inevitably he was persuaded to take on a political leadership role to which he was manifestly unsuited. And he knew it. He had never previously attended meetings or conferences, he had not been to any Zionist Congresses and was never happy with open democratic activities. He abhorred politics and politicians, especially those operating in the international arena. He held that instead of engaging in discussions about the future with Governments around the world, they should be undertaking real work on the ground in Palestine or persuading others to support that work. It was this negative view of Weizmann and the Zionist Organization that led him to his life-long antipathy to their activities. Jews of the Yishuv (the resident Jewish population) felt distant and unrepresented by the Zionist Organization based in London while the local Zionist Organisation officials in Palestine, headed by Colonel Kisch, seemed little better (*Fig. 30*). His opinion happened to coincide with that of many in the Yishuv and it was why they now turned to one of their own, a man of action, and away from the Zionist Organisation.

Figure 30: Colonel Frederick Kisch, Zionist Organization leader in Palestine

The Arab riots of 1929 shook the Administration and revealed the disorganisation and lack of leadership amongst the Jewish population. A representative body, the Va'ad HaLeumi, (Jewish National Council), had been set up in 1920 to bring together various factions in an elected Assembly with a smaller executive body. It met about once a year and focussed on internal affairs. It was not regarded as effective by the Administration and, in 1929, the High Commissioner, Sir John Chancellor, was saying that he found it less than helpful. The Jewish population was not enamoured by it either. The successes of Rutenberg stood out in contrast; he had many prized attributes that made him appealing. While he had never belonged to any political party, his background in socialism made him attractive to the workers and his success in business commended him to the capitalists. A man of the people with a pride in order and discipline made him popular with his workforce, at least for the moment, and his ready access to the High Commissioner in Palestine and to Ministers and officials in the Colonial Office in London were seen as considerable assets. Despite their disagreements, Chancellor admired Rutenberg and often turned to him for advice and support.

Two examples suffice. Would he speak to his friend the Chief Rabbi Kook about the practice of blowing the Shofar, the ram's horn, at the Western Wall at the end of the service on Yom Kipur? This was always a flash point for the Muslims whose Al Aqsa Mosque lay immediately adjacent to the Wall on the Holy Mount and the Shofar was said by them to be causing a disturbance. Rutenberg was not in the least religious and had not attended a synagogue since early childhood, but admired and respected Chief Rabbi Kook. Much later he rebuilt a religious seminary (Yeshiva b'Yavneh) in Kook's honour. He eventually came to a satisfactory compromise in which the Shofar could be blown at a separate site. Of course, that was not the end of the many disputes around the Western Wall, but for the moment Chancellor was satisfied.

The other example occurred when the Jewish workers of the Histradut (Trade Union) came into conflict with their employers, the Department for Public Works, during the construction of the port at Haifa. Rutenberg was heavily involved in the port construction and had been supplying electricity there. The new dispute centred around the need to avoid work on the Sabbath and, inevitably, on wages. Chancellor did not hesitate to ask Rutenberg to intervene and sort it out. This he did with the minimum of fuss and no publicity. His efforts in settling the dispute in Haifa had even reached the ears of the Colonial Office in London. Less was known at the time about his dictatorial form of paternalism and his disregard for the Trade Union movement. He prevented his own workers from joining the Union.

Chancellor clearly regarded him as the man to go to when he needed a mediator in any local disputes.

Now there was the crisis of the Arab riots of August 1929 that highlighted a Jewish leadership that had been wooed into complacency by several years of seemingly peaceful relationships. It was little wonder that the Va'ad HaLeumi turned to Rutenberg. For the moment at least, his overbearing attitudes and lack of sympathy for democratic principles seemed less of a problem. Perhaps too, they were unaware that, when he had been in America in 1915, he had resisted the idea that the views of the Jewish public there might be taken into account when he was involved in the foundation of the Jewish Congress Movement. He much preferred to simply accept the private opinions of the leaders of the various factions.

He was never someone to take the opinions of the public seriously and the Va'ad soon knew that the man they appointed was no democrat.

The question arises as to why Rutenberg agreed to take on an essentially political role when he had so frequently expressed such aversion to politics? The answer may lie in part in how he defined 'politics'. It was 'democratic' politics and 'party' politics that he found so difficult.

He watched with growing angst, the endless back-biting debates amongst the Zionists at their Congresses, where personal rivalries were fought out for prestige and reputation, and where, according to him, so little that was practical was achieved. His type of politics involved quiet, personal discussions with decision-making power-brokers behind closed doors. He abhorred publicity and believed that the masses did not even need to be consulted. He had probably gained some of these views on governance from his time as a revolutionary in Russia. He felt that the ignorant peasantry there was too suppressed to have its own opinions and only needed actions to be taken for it and not by it. He had never been in the political wing of the Socialist Revolutionary Party, only in the wing concerned with 'action'. Those are the attitudes he displayed as he took on the leadership of the Va'ad HaLeumi. He immediately set the course for complete control.

Firstly, he was at pains to prevent the media reporting his appointment as Chairman. From then on, he allowed very limited access to the press and then only directly through him. He rode over the objections of the Executive Committee, he suggested that it was too large, and followed that by appointing a small number of members who would be loyal and responsible only to him. He reformed the local, area, committee structure by putting his own people in as leaders. If this smacks of dictatorship, then that is certainly what he intended. He had little patience with fruitless debates and questioning of decisions. His early flirtation with totalitarian communism and his later friendship with Mussolini seem all of a pattern. He then began to burnish the image of the organisation. To impress visitors, he changed the premises from those from which they had hitherto operated. He ensured that he and his senior colleagues were invited to ceremonial and social events and he centralised the workings of the institution. And he threatened to walk away if his erstwhile colleagues did not accept his proposals. The fear of losing him made them swallow hard and accept his strictures. He was adamant that the Va'ad should take on the oversight of health and education, much to the chagrin of Colonel Kisch. It mattered little to Rutenberg that formal permission from the Zionist Organisation to take on these responsibilities was not granted until 1932, long after he had left office. He simply took them on immediately. Kisch was constantly trying to raise barriers to Rutenberg's endeavours but, never one to await officialdom, he extended the reach of the Va'ad HaLeumi into public and road building services, and social care. Kisch was incandescent when he heard that Rutenberg was intent on writing directly to the Mandate Commission of the League of Nations when it was way beyond his level of responsibility. It was the Zionist Organisation that was the sole body that had been agreed to represent Jewish opinion. So now Rutenberg was in a constant struggle not only with his fellow Va'ad HaLeumi executive members but also with the Zionist Organisation in Palestine.

But it was when he ventured into the political arena of Arab-Jewish relations where he found even more resistance. Not unreasonably he felt that the Jews of the Yishuv knew better than the Z.O. in London how to deal with the Arabs. Indeed, he believed that no-one knew better than he himself. Although others on his executive, especially his friend Harry Sacher, thought otherwise, he pressed on with direct dealings with those Arabs whom he thought opposed the line taken by their leaders. Using bribery, he tried to curry favour with some in Jaffa and spent time trying to woo Rageb Nashashibi, a rival to the Husseini family. The latter included the Grand Mufti, Haj Amin al Husseini, a formidable opponent of Jewish endeavours. Rutenberg also regarded security arrangements and settlement policy as aspects of governance that the Va'ad HaLeumi was fully capable of pursuing without too much reference to the Zionist leadership. He was raising more hackles and all this left Colonel Kisch even more irate as he entered further into the province of the Zionist Organization. At one stage he had a hard time convincing them to rebuild the Jewish community in Hebron after the riots of 1929.

They were resistant on the grounds that it was too isolated a community and difficult to defend against the surrounding Arab villages. He was irritated by their lack of foresight.

Despite his abiding concern and deep involvement in his work in Palestine, he recognised that the centre of influence lay in London. He rushed home from there in September 1929 when he became aware that the leadership of the Va'ad HaLeumi awaited him, but he returned to London in November 1929 and again in March 1930. He was only in Palestine for a few weeks between those dates and had taken time out to recuperate in St. Moritz on his way home. He was beginning to feel the mental and physical stress of the many painful debates and disagreements with which he was faced.

He found himself losing control in the political quagmire of London. To some extent he was able to float above the internal squabbles of the Zionists and, on at least two occasions, he was called upon to act as a 'neutral' mediator. Ultimately, however, he was unsuccessful in convincing the Government that his particular plans for Palestine were acceptable, and he retired hurt. It was not due to his efforts that the dream of a Jewish homeland survived. That depended on political factors well outside his control. The next Chapter deals with some of these traumatic times for Rutenberg and for the Jews.

CHAPTER 19

Striving for national unity

Already in September 1929, Rutenberg knew that more would be needed to keep the Arab-Jewish conflict from erupting further, and he was pressing Ministers for stronger action to keep control of Arab militant activities. The Jews were barely recovering from the death and destruction of the July riots that had had created such a serious sense of insecurity. He was fully aware, as he rushed home on the 9th, that this was a moment when national unity was desperately needed as the chasm between Arabs and Jews deepened.

Rutenberg had had many formal and informal discussions with High Commissioner Chancellor, about the deteriorating relations between Arabs and Jews. In contrast, Zionist officials in Palestine only rarely had the opportunity of meetings with the High Commissioner. But Chancellor thought Rutenberg might be useful to him as a counterweight to the Zionist officials. Although suspicious, and rarely actually agreeing with him, he believed that Rutenberg might help him. He thought that by taking the Yishuv out of the hands of the Z.O., Rutenberg would help give the Arabs a greater say in the governance of Palestine. Although Rutenberg did support open discussion with the Arabs, and, as we will see, his paper for the Colonial Office showed him to be more open than most to compromise, everything he introduced had its limitations.

But it says something for his facility to bamboozle, at times, those with whom he dealt.

Regarding the Arabs, Chancellor continually pressed for their increased representation in the governance of Palestine. An Executive Council, with strong Arab membership was part of a solution he particularly favoured and the Colonial Office under Lord Passfield was to be similarly inclined.

Setting off for London in November 1929, Rutenberg was well aware that there was little appetite amongst the Yishuv for offering the Arabs any more concessions after the uprising when so many Jews had been slaughtered in Hebron, Safed and Jerusalem. Now there was a hiccup as Weizmann and Kisch misunderstood Rutenberg's position on a peace initiative with the Arabs. This had been raised by Judah Magnes, the American Rabbi and now Chancellor of the Hebrew University in Jerusalem (*Fig. 31*). He and Colonel H St. John Philby had concocted a plan that included a governing body constituted purely according to the size of each population. Magnes believed that only by giving the Arabs their full democratic rights could peace occur, and

Figure 31: Judah Magnes, President, Hebrew University and peace activist

that the Jews should take the high moral ground no matter how damaging it might be to their aspirations for a Jewish homeland. His views were not popular amongst Jews so recently the subject of an Arab killing spree. Philby had been advisor to King Ibn Saud, later as Political Secretary in Iraq and more recently British Representative in Trans-Jordan, but had fallen out of favour with Whitehall over British policy. He had converted to Islam and when he turned up in Jerusalem, Magnes was attracted to his ideas. They began presenting their peace plans to the High Commissioner and to officials in London.

Now Rutenberg became entangled. It is interesting to examine how a man with such forthright views as Rutenberg was to become involved with Magnes while he was entirely opposed to the Magnes/Philby plan. Indeed he had a quite different idea on how to deal with Arabs. At a meeting with Magnes and the High Commissioner, Rutenberg did not mince his words. When Chancellor asked him what he would do to improve the situation for the Arabs Rutenberg said, 'with bayonets!' He constantly pressed for a much stronger response with an increase in the numbers of police and troops. He said he knew from experience that the Arab in the street was content to rub along peaceably with the Jews. It was their leaders who were so vile. His view was that you cannot trust the Arab leadership and if they cannot be controlled 'with bayonets' it had to be with 'bribes'. Needless to say, this attitude grated with Chancellor; but it did not prevent him appreciating Rutenberg's contributions nor did it stop him calling on him for help.

While the Magnes suggestion, taken up by Chancellor, that the Balfour Declaration should be revisited was clearly something that Rutenberg would never abide, it did not mean that he was ignorant of the Arabs needs or that they should be given more. And Rutenberg's opposition to Magnes's peace plans did not interfere with the mutual respect they felt for each other. Magnes had, for example, tried to persuade American donors to cough up for Rutenberg's electrification project. And Rutenberg certainly believed in full and open discussion with the Arabs. Indeed, he felt strongly that there was a need for much better Arab-Jewish relations. Both he and Magnes had the same aim, but they differed widely in how to achieve it.

Rutenberg seemed able to disagree without complete alienation when it suited him and, as we will see, he incorporated some of the Magnes ideas in a paper he later presented to the Colonial Office.

But on his relationship with Magnes, Weizmann certainly grabbed the wrong end of Rutenberg's stick. Weizmann, and his man in Jerusalem Colonel Kisch, were sensitised to Rutenberg's interference, so when he arrived on the scene in London, they were persuaded that he had been taken in by Magnes's peace initiative and that he would undermine all their efforts. Nothing was further from the truth but their suspicions were not assuaged. It was they who were in charge of delicate negotiations with Ministers and officials in the Colonial and Foreign Offices. Or so they believed. They were trying to negotiate a better arrangement with the Government and were inclined to accept, at least in part, the idea of a type of Executive Agency in Palestine. They did not want to see their pitch queered by a Magnes-type deal that they believed Rutenberg was sponsoring.

Relations between Rutenberg and Weizmann were always poor but Berl Katznelson, friendly with both, did manage to bring about a partial reconciliation. Katznelson was one of the founders of the labour trade union, Histradut, and a strong advocate for peaceful co-existence with the Arabs. And for a short while co-existence between Weizmann and Rutenberg improved too. But Weizmann only slowly lost the perception that Rutenberg was sold on the Magnes/Philby plan and had not quite grasped that Rutenberg was capable of disagreement without loss of his respect for Magnes. Meanwhile Magnes was making himself increasingly unpopular in the Hebrew University in Jerusalem. Students heckled his pro-Arab speeches and the staff rapidly became unhappy with the views he was preaching. The university administration then arranged for his 'promotion' to the Presidency where he no longer had an administrative role and was out of harm's way.

In London, arguments with the Zionist Organization about who should have supremacy in presenting the Jewish case were vocal and frequent. An extended 'Jewish Agency' had recently been instituted at the Zionist Congress in Zurich and its membership enlarged to include serious and senior international figures including Albert Einstein, Leon Blum, Lord Melchett, Arthur Balfour and, from America, Louis Marshall and Felix Warburg. This 'Jewish Agency' was responsible at the interface between the diaspora and the Jews of Palestine. It was to raise awareness and support for the Homeland and encourage funding as well as immigration.

Here was another body into whose territory Rutenberg was beginning to stray; another body that he regarded as completely unnecessary, for him to joust with. There is little doubt that he resembled a loose cannon as he fired off in all directions much to the distress of the Z.O. He certainly did not mince his words when he met Sir John Shuckburgh or his Colonial Secretary, Lord Passfield, in January 1930.

His view was that the Arab population at large had no appetite for self-government and was, in any event, quite incapable of achieving it. Rutenberg as usual was pressing for firmer action against the Arab leadership. According to him, strong tactics were needed, troops were being withdrawn too quickly and the vacuum in the defence of the Jews should be repaired as quickly as possible. In making his case, Rutenberg was effectively undermining the position of the High Commissioner in Jerusalem. In vain did his friend Harry Sacher warn him that he was sacrificing his good relationship with Chancellor. Sacher supported him on most issues but on this he parted company. It mattered little to Rutenberg that Sacher may have been correct about his alienation of Chancellor, but it is unlikely to have done much to worsen the latter's firm anti-Zionist stance.

Unfortunately for Rutenberg his bid for more troops to control Arab uprisings fell on deaf ears. The Colonial Office was hell-bent on reducing costs in the Middle East and it was only very much later that they were forced to send in the army.

Rutenberg was beginning to tire under the barrage of criticism he was receiving from his Va'ad HaLeumi colleagues and the Zionists in London and was threatening, once again, to resign. He had bounced back after recuperating in St Moritz in February, but the threat of resignation was a ploy he used more than once in later years.

At this stage he was writing to his colleagues that he was making progress with the Colonial Office but was less than happy with the 'internal arguments and anarchy' in the Z.O. and Jewish Agency.

The Jewish Agency, as usual with Jewish organisations, found much room for disagreement with other bodies and even within its own membership. Einstein could not get along with Weizmann and his ideas about the future of a Jewish Palestine. Felix Warburg, representing American opinion, tended towards Rutenberg's view that Palestine was a land in which to invest and build while the Zionists were seeking international political support and philanthropy. Nor was Weizmann entirely pleased with the way the Jewish Agency were undermining his authority. Disagreements between the American faction and allies of Weizmann reached such a pitch that they took the remarkable step of asking Rutenberg to help in reconciliation, something they were to do again a little later.

He, being considered neutral, was tasked with going to America to seek a resolution. He turned down the American trip, probably because of pressure from the Chairman of his Electric Company, Lord Reading, who reminded him of his prime responsibilities to the Company. But it says something about the turmoil amongst the Jewish representatives milling around in London during 1930 that they turned to someone who was nothing if not controversial. If we need reminding that he was considered a man of influence, the ease with which he gained an audience with Government Ministers makes it difficult to forget.

The Jewish Agency and the Z.O. did eventually come together in a conciliatory approach to the Arab question in the belief that they could head off stronger stringencies being applied by a Government increasingly more in sympathy with the Arabs than the Jews.

The Government's first Commission of Inquiry, the 'Shaw Report', on the disturbances in Palestine was published in March 1930, and the Zionists were doing their best to influence its impact. It is worth examining the background to this, and a later, second, Commission of Inquiry, plus the White Paper that followed, and the ways in which Rutenberg became fully involved.

The disturbances following prayers at the Western Wall in August 1929 simply lit the fuse and the full-blown riots that followed saw widespread death and destruction throughout Palestine. It was inevitable that there would be Government-inspired inquiries and two of these were published during 1930. Weizmann tried hard to constrain the remit of the first, the 'Shaw Inquiry', to little avail. I have written previously about the details of these inquiries.*

---

* *Mandate. The Palestine Crucible, 1919-1939.* Leslie Turnberg. 1921. Vallentine Mitchell, London.

Here I will simply report their conclusions. The remit of the first Inquiry was to restrict itself to the immediate cause of the riots, a religious disturbance, and specifically to exclude reference to wider political factors. The limitations placed on the Commission were ignored when it ascribed the underlying cause to Arab fears of being overwhelmed by uncontrolled Jewish immigration and the loss of their land. Furthermore, it ventured even further into the political arena when it recommended more action be taken to control these supposed causal factors. It mattered little that Henry Snell, the Labour M.P. member of the Commission, disagreed with the conclusions of the Report and wrote a minority opinion in which he denied the main conclusion that the riots were caused by Jewish immigration. He went on to argue that the main culprit for the riots was the Grand Mufti.

When the Shaw Commission Report was published in March, the Zionists tried to head off its recommendations. Rutenberg pressed for more concerted action and suggested publicising their vocal protests amongst world Jewry. An executive group was formed with the Jewish Agency and although Rutenberg refused to become a member as representative of the Va'ad HaLeumi, he joined as an observer and went on to head a subcommittee for propaganda and policy formulation.

The Prime Minister, Ramsay MacDonald, was distracted by innumerable domestic political matters but agreed to meet Jewish representatives, including Weizmann, Lord Melchett, Lord Reading, James de Rothschild and Rutenberg.

Shuckburgh and Passfield were there to hear the case too but nothing was promised. MacDonald wanted to be shot of the whole Palestine affair and hoped the Arabs and Jews could settle their differences themselves.

A report of the Shaw Commission now had to be presented to the Mandate Commission of the League of Nations and Weizmann and the Zionist Executive were alarmed at the direction it was taking. They became even more distressed when the team appointed to present the findings was announced. It included Harry Luke, whom they reviled because of his inaction in Jerusalem during the riots, T I K Lloyd, who had been Secretary to the despised Shaw Commission Report and Drummond-Shields, an Under Secretary in the Colonial Office. The fact that Snell's minority opinion on Shaw's Report was ignored in their presentation to the Mandate Commission did little to assuage the Zionists' suspicions of bias.

The Government needed a more thorough examination of the impact of immigration on the Arab population and a full analysis of the available land. Weizmann suggested that they appoint General Jan Smuts, a friend of the Zionists, for the job but Passfield refused and appointed Sir John Hope-Simpson instead.

Weizmann, already unhappy with the way in which he felt he was being treated by the Government, became personally affronted by Passfield's action. He decided on a course of non-co-operation and refused to talk to Passfield, although secretly maintaining contact with the Prime Minister through his son, Malcolm MacDonald. More significantly he turned to Rutenberg to continue to negotiate with the Colonial Office.

Rutenberg had come away with the idea that there was room for movement by the Government and it was in his position as a 'neutral' that he agreed to meet Lord Passfield (*Fig. 32*). He prepared well and met him with a fully worked-up document. He had already travelled to Paris on the 17th of May to gain Baron Rothschild's approval, particularly for the economic aspects of his proposals. And he had had several meetings with Sir John Shuckburgh of the Colonial Office who, although he found Rutenberg's manner overbearing, remained impressed by his ideas. Rutenberg had demanded immediate access to the Prime Minister the following morning and Shuckburgh had to bring him down to earth. He eventually overcame his reservations about the pushy Rutenberg and his ideas.

Figure 32: Lord Passfield (Sidney Webb), Socialist Secretary of State in the Colonial Office and author of the 1930 'White Paper'

It was a remarkably far-sighted set of proposals that Rutenberg managed to present to both the Colonial Secretary and the Prime Minister.

Passfield was suspicious and gave little away as he stared at Pinchas. Stroking his beard he steadied himself for what he thought would be another Rutenberg onslaught. His posture was not encouraging but he was surprised as Pinchas seemed to lean over backwards to be accommodating. He was about to offer the Arabs a future in the development of the country. Rutenberg launched into his eight point plan, the main messages of which were: separate Jewish and Arab democratically elected national bodies; a joint Advisory Committee for matters concerning both Arabs and Jews under the Chairmanship of the Chief Secretary; immigration to be limited by the economic absorptive capacity of the country; and land purchase to be authorised by the Government with compensation for tenant Fellahin and land owners.

Then came the bid for the Government to renew their commitment to the Jewish National home. The Palestine Administration should be reorganised so that its personnel were 'in sympathy with the Jewish National Home Policy'. Here he was pointing at Harry Luke, the High Commissioner's deputy left in charge during the riots and whom he believed to be out of sympathy with the Jews. He pressed for censorship of the press against racial and religious incitement and a 'clean sweep of communists, both Jews and Arabs'. Here he was betraying his belief that it was external Bolshevik influences that were inciting the Arab revolt. Finally, he wanted to see the Prime Minister make a public statement confirming the Jewish National Home policy, 'and expressing appreciation of the Jewish achievements in Palestine (this to counter-balance the depressing effect of the Shaw Report on Jewish public opinion)'.

There was one other matter that he slipped in and to which we will return. Ever the entrepreneur and businessman, he sought a loan of £1 million, jointly with the Emir Abdullah, to assist the Arabs in the development of Trans-Jordan. It was his long-term dream to improve the economy of Jordan and in so doing, improve relations between the Jews and the Emir Abdullah. Passfield expressed some interest. Sadly, the timing was far from conducive to an agreement; Passfield was considering further restrictions on the Jews that were to emerge a little later in his White Paper.

But this was indeed an impressive set of proposals, and Shuckburgh was enthusiastic in presenting them to Passfield.

He may even have helped Rutenberg with the wording but wanted to check whether he was out of step with opinion in the Jewish Agency and the Zionist Executive. The Executive was certainly worried by Weizmann's attitude of non-cooperation with the Government and were unaware and uncertain about what Rutenberg was up to. It was typical that Rutenberg shared the contents of his paper only belatedly with the Zionist Executive and, with the Va'ad HaLeumi, just a day or so after he made his presentation to Passfield on the 22nd of May. Interestingly he may have consulted Magnes on some of the points he was making, and Weizmann had probably nodded it through so far as he was aware of its contents.

His offer of a self-governing body for the Arabs, alongside one for the Jews, was one that the Arabs had found unacceptable on more than one occasion and continued to do so, but for Rutenberg to suggest it was a surprise to Passfield. The proposal to seek funds to compensate tenants losing their land was farsighted and something Rutenberg himself was already practicing as he acquired land for his electricity plants. His idea that Trans-Jordan should receive development funds was visionary.

Of course, he had been pressing for some years for greater access to Trans-Jordan to expand his electrification scheme. He had had friendly discussions with the Emir Abdullah about investment in the development of his country. Impoverished and tempted by Rutenberg's blandishments he had not been entirely averse to personal bribes. Now, in 1930, Rutenberg was proposing that the UK Government invest to the tune of £1million in Trans-Jordan and, in so doing, helping alleviate the conditions of the Fellahin, deprived of their land in Palestine, by offering a country in which they could settle, east of the Jordan River.

He had always placed much faith in his ability to convince at least some of the Arabs to come over to his views. He had met a number during their stay in London and had even attempted to bribe Nashashibi to oil the wheels. But he was placing too much reliance on his power to influence intractable Arab opinion at home. Rutenberg, as ever, wanted to keep his name out of any publicity for this scheme and pressed those he told of it to keep his role secret. It should be seen by the Arabs, and Jews, entirely as a British Government proposal, and not just another Rutenberg scheme, if it was to stand any chance of being accepted. Neither did he want the High Commissioner, whom he knew would object, to be told of its contents until much later.

Passfield and the Prime Minister had both been momentarily impressed when they met Rutenberg. MacDonald's dark eyes had lit up when faced with a Jew with interesting ideas. Passfield had given him a preview of Rutenberg's proposals and now he was even more taken with a characteristic

Rutenberg presentation. Here was a call for positive Government action in contrast to the complaints and carping criticisms of the Zionists. Passfield knew that the Arab delegation then in London had shown complete opposition to any deal that involved the Jews having a say in the governance of Palestine, but he was at least partially convinced by Rutenberg that they did not necessarily represent Arab feeling at home. Perhaps Rutenberg could work his magic on them through the Nashashibi family, the rivals to the Husseini faction? It was with that hope in mind that Passfield sent two telegrams to Chancellor in Jerusalem with an outline of the Rutenberg proposals while mentioning Rutenberg's authorship only in the second, personal, telegram.

It was then that the Rutenberg's proposals hit a brick wall.

Chancellor immediately rejected the whole idea. Two separate governing bodies were a recipe for confusion and disarray. It would cement the division of the two communities who should be more concerned with living together. The Arabs would never agree to it and now was quite the wrong time, while Hope-Simpson was busily making his Inquiry in Palestine. Chancellor placed much confidence in Hope-Simpson and was keen to support the direction he was beginning to take against Jewish immigration. His response to Passfield was clear, if diplomatically worded. But his letter to his son at the same time was less so. It betrayed his strong antipathy to Zionist aims and suggested he would resign if Rutenberg's proposals were accepted.

The fact that Rutenberg's suggestions may not have been fully supported by Weizmann's colleagues caused the Colonial

Office some concern too but, in the end, it mattered little in the face of the High Commissioner's rejection.

The near fatal Hope-Simpson's Inquiry Report was soon to follow.

News of what it would contain had already reached the Colonial Office in telegrams from Hope-Simpson in June and July. He was even then pressing for strict limitations on immigration and land purchase. In this he was in cahoots with Chancellor who had very similar views. Rutenberg had had a meeting with Prime Minister MacDonald on July 15th, at which he laid out his plan at great length, while MacDonald could do little but listen quietly. Meanwhile Chancellor had arrived in London to put a spanner in Rutenberg's works. Now Passfield and the Prime Minister went into reverse on Rutenberg's eight-point plan. Chancellor's case was made on the basis of, what to him, was the certain refusal by the Arabs to accept the plan. He pointed out that since it was entirely dependent on Arab acceptance it was no-longer viable. Passfield, who had also placed some confidence on the idea of a deal with Abdullah of Trans-Jordan, now simply turned tail. They must await Hope-Simpson's full Report and not do anything to upset the Arabs in the meanwhile. It was Chancellor versus Rutenberg, and Rutenberg lost.

There were indeed many weaknesses in Rutenberg's case. His erstwhile Zionist colleagues were far from uniformly supportive but, more importantly, he over-estimated his capacity to convince the Arabs and their responses to his bribery techniques were less than fulsome. He had made himself believe that a combination of British resolve to clamp down on Arab uprisings and his bribes would win them over. But he reckoned without the determination of Haj Amin al Husseini and his followers. The final nail in the coffin was driven in by Chancellor, and now Passfield and the Prime Minister became convinced of the strength of Arab opposition.

October saw the publication of Hope-Simpson's long anticipated Report. Its conclusion provoked little surprise. There was no more land available for Jewish immigrants while Arab agricultural workers still needed it for themselves. Hope-Simpson had gathered a huge amount of data about the nature of the land, and what he took to be its capacity for agricultural development, and about the Arab requirements for land that they could cultivate. The fact that his data were soon shown to be grossly flawed did not deter him from publishing them as if they were factually correct, nor did it stop Passfield from accepting them in full.

CHAPTER 20

The Passfield 'White Paper'

In October 1930, Passfield went ahead and published his 'White Paper' simultaneously with Hope-Simpson's Report.

Then came their simple and devastating message. Balfour's Declaration was to be orientated away from the promise to 'view with favour the establishment in Palestine of a national home for the Jewish people' and towards 'nothing shall be done which may prejudice the civil and religious rights of existing non-Jewish communities in Palestine'. Jewish immigration should be severely curtailed and purchase of land prohibited. The Arab press was elated; 'Balfour was dead'. But not yet buried according to Husseini who wanted more.

Uproar followed. Weizmann resigned from the Z.O., there were demonstrations in New York, letters to the Press from Peers and ex-Ministers and the minority Labour Government of Ramsay MacDonald felt threatened at a moment when they needed the distraction the least. Ben Gurion, as leader of the Jewish Labour movement, mobilised his resources and was invited to meet MacDonald at Chequers to try to rescue the decisions. Rutenberg had been unable to influence the impact of the earlier Shaw Report, but he was now trying to stir things up with his influential friends, Lord Melchett, Lord Reading and H Snell, M.P., by persuading them to take up the cudgels on behalf of the Zionists. It was the pressure to do something immediately to stop immigration that was causing most angst. In vain did Shuckburgh tried to rescue part of Rutenberg's original proposal. He pointed to the clauses that suggested that immigration should be limited to absorptive capacity and controlled by the High Commissioner, while land transfer arrangements should be closely linked to recompense in money or land elsewhere. But, in isolation from all his other proposals, Rutenberg would have nothing to do with limits on immigration or land purchase. It was all or nothing for him even though he had had a hard time convincing the Jewish Agency Executive of his proposals. Their reluctance had the unfortunate effect of undermining Rutenberg in the eyes of the Colonial Office, and playing into the hands of Chancellor.

Sadly, Rutenberg's proposals were then completely forgotten. They re-emerged from time to time in various guises but for now they were a dead letter. It might have saved much misery for the Zionists and many headaches for the British Administration if Rutenberg's eight-point proposal had been introduced before the Arab riots of 1929. It is conceivable that it could have formed the basis of an agreement of which both Arabs and Jews might have approved. But against that is the fact that the Grand Mufti Husseini never, at any time then or in the future, agreed to any proposal that included involvement of the Jews in the future of Palestine.

Rutenberg had tried hard but neither he nor the more politically astute Ben Gurion and Weizmann had prevented the outcome and they were now working hard to mitigate the damage. Ultimately, however, it was less their pressure than a series of simultaneous political events that determined the ways in which the Zionists were rescued for the moment.

The reasons why the Government eventually backtracked on their 'White Paper' were complicated and only partly due to the pressure of the Jews. MacDonald's minority Labour Government was vulnerable to a by-election in the East End of London, with its huge Jewish population, and he needed to keep the Jews on-side if they were to retain the seat. One surprising British figure who proved helpful in mobilising Labour Party support for the Zionists was Ernest Bevin, General Secretary of the powerful Transport and General Workers Union. It was the same Bevin who later, as Foreign Secretary, vociferously opposed the creation of the State of Israel in 1947 and 1948.

There was the need too, to get Palestine off the Cabinet's agenda which was dominated by the much bigger problem of Indian pressure for independence. The Liberal and Conservative parties were snapping at the heels of MacDonald's Government about India, and he decided to ask his Foreign Secretary, Arthur Henderson, a friend of the Jews, to examine the whole issue again. Henderson had been in Lloyd George's war time Cabinet that had issued the Balfour Declaration and he now consulted Weizmann in writing his report. Here was a manifestation of MacDonald's need to shift responsibility from Passfield, who was proving a political embarrassment at the Colonial Office, to the Foreign Office.

Given the task of examining the fallout, Henderson was in a desperate rush as he was busy working on a peace and disarmament initiative for the League of Nations (for which he was later given the Nobel Peace Prize) and he did not need this distraction. His report was helpful in giving MacDonald a way out. MacDonald retreated and issued what the Arabs termed the 'Black Letter' that softened the blow by 're-interpreting' the Passfield message. It was written as a letter to Weizmann and reported to Parliament 'in order to remove certain misconceptions and misunderstandings'. There was no way the Government would renege on its promises to the Jews. The Government was under 'international obligations from which there was no question of receding'.

For the time being the Zionists' dream of a National Home had survived. Immigration and land purchase continued but the Jews were shaken and increasingly wary of the Government's motives and actions.

The Arabs were dismayed, and High Commissioner Chancellor was extremely disappointed with the outcome. He had been hoping for more for the Arabs.

And as for Rutenberg, the future relationship between Arabs and Jews was not the only topic where he was seen to be stepping on the toes of the Z.O. Unfortunately for him, he was to get little further with his plans for a 'Great Holding Company' to support his industrial investment ideas.

Hitherto the Va'ad HaLeumi had subsisted on handouts from the Zionist Organization. Rutenberg had a grand plan to raise a sinking fund of £5 million to £10 million to take on a great deal of public work independent from the Zionist Organization but this now fell off the table. Nor did he get his

£1 million from the Government to support developments in Trans-Jordan. He put the idea to his confidante, Lord Reading, who was anything but enthusiastic. Reading could not see any philanthropists willing to donate such large funds to an unstable country in trouble. Nor did Rutenberg receive any support from the High Commissioner or his good friend Harry Sacher. While that did not put him off, in the end he was unsuccessful in raising his money.

In all his dealings Rutenberg had betrayed his suspicions of nationalism, whether it be Zionism or Palestinian Nationalism. An internationalist from his early revolutionary days he wanted to see national borders bypassed by economic investment that would encourage a more cosmopolitan world. He had little time for narrow nationalists, even Jewish nationalists, in his expansionist ideology. It was to his misfortunate that he underestimated the power of nationalism in the Middle East while over-estimating the value of bribery.

Rutenberg returned with even grander ideas much later, in 1939, when he presented the case for the 'Economic Development of a Federation of Syria, Lebanon, Trans-Jordan, Iraq and Palestine'. It was a 'Common Market' for the Middle East. No doubt he would have been fascinated by the potential for trade collaboration opened up by the 'Abraham Accords' between the United Arab Emirates, Bahrain and Israel in 2020. Sadly, in 1939 the time was not right for such far-sighted initiatives. In London, on the verge of a world war, the British Government found the idea much too radical. By then Rutenberg too was more concerned by the rise of Hitler and what that would mean for the Jews of Europe.

In July 1930 Rutenberg was losing heart. The rejection of his plans by Passfield and the Prime Minister was enough to see him depressed and weakened. Completely disillusioned, he decided there and then to resign from all political activity and return to his comfort zone in hydro-electricity. His tenuous belief in the value of politics and political declarations as a means of achieving anything of value for the Jews of Palestine was now broken. Only work on the ground could achieve success and anything that could be done to maintain a supply of funds for that end was worth the effort. Hitherto he had avoided criticising Weizmann and the Jewish Agency too strongly. Now an independent critic, he was free to say what he liked and from then on he did not hide his disagreements from the Zionist Organisation. He even threatened to withdraw from the leadership of the Va'ad HaLeumi, but held on while he took some time out for rest and recuperation on his way home. He left London on the 23rd of July, shortly after his meeting with Passfield, and stopped off on his way in Paris. There he met Baron Rothschild and Felix Warburg whom he still valued as being in tune with his ideas of what the Yishuv needed.

At this point he seemed a broken man. But any idea that he was a spent force would soon be dismissed. He spent five weeks recuperating in Switzerland and only reached Palestine on the 9th of September. Even then he bypassed the Va'ad HaLeumi executive, travelling straight to the welcome respite of his hydro-electricity plant on the Jordan River. He did eventually address his Executive Committee a few days later when, for the first time, he gave them a lengthy description, in secret, of what he had been up to in London. It was biased in his derogatory comments about the ineptitude of Weizmann, the London Zionists and the Jewish Agency, while fully justifying his own role. He was scathing about Chancellor's role and never ceased blaming the UK Government for failing to see the value of his ideas. He felt strongly that the Government was making a big mistake in believing that the Arabs were united in opposition to the Zionists while he 'knew' that it was only the small, violent, leading minority who were the real enemy. If they could be controlled the rest would come round as economic development progressed. And if the Government gave way to a minority of Arabs, the 15 millions of world Jewry would never forgive them. Of course, he knew he had failed to convince the Government of the logic of his arguments as he saw it. And now he did not convince his executive, who were beginning to be disillusioned by his leadership. He was also tiring of the constant sniping and said he would be resigning in October. Under pressure, he put it off for a few months until he finally left office in January 1931, a disillusioned man but one who was now free to focus on his first love at Naharayim.

CHAPTER 21

More initiatives

Rutenberg had his hydro-electric plant fully operational by 1932 and now, an established entrepreneur and relatively free of political responsibilities, his restless spirit left him casting round for yet more challenges.

His appetite for new ventures was undiminished and, with a clear eye for the future in 1934, he recognised that aviation was becoming a critically important driver for prosperity. He began negotiating with the British Air Ministry to develop a commercial airline in Palestine, and with the support of the Jewish Agency and Histradut he established the Palestinian Airways company. He had gained the technical support of Britain's Imperial Airways and opened for business in July 1934 (*Fig. 33*). His Palestinian Airways was taken over by Imperial Airways in 1937 and, because of the danger of Arab hostilities around Lydda, a new airport was opened at Sde Dov in Tel Aviv. Initially flying three times a week from Haifa to Tel Aviv, it later extended its flights to Beirut and by 1939 was flying twice a day. Haifa-

Figure 33: Palestine Airways aeroplane

Tel Aviv flights took 35 minutes and cost LS 1,000 one way and LS 1,800 return. There were enough paying customers to make it a viable commercial proposition.

Rutenberg saw the birth of his creation but by 1940, as the war with Germany evolved, the Royal Air Force took over the airport and all the airplanes for their military operations. At the end of the war the Airways were returned to commercial use and by 1947 formed the basis of Israel's Defence Force as well as El Al. By then Rutenberg was no longer alive.

He continued his running battle with individuals in the Jewish Agency who were critical of him and the way he operated outside their control. But he was still regarded as a heroic figure within the Yishuv.

He became involved in yet another dispute when the Jewish Agency tried to drain the Hula lake and swamp north of his Jordan River plant, and use the land for the thousands of new immigrants expected to arrive each year. Having purchased the lake from the Salim brothers of Beirut, the Zionist Organisation discovered that reclamation of the land was prohibitively expensive. Furthermore, it would only support some 2,000 new homes. Rutenberg had other suggestions. He was still pressing the idea that much more land could be made available for immigrants in Trans-Jordan than in the Hula Valley. But of more immediate importance to him in 1936 was the fear that draining the Hula lake would deprive him of water for his Jordan River generator. The waters of the Hula drained into Lake Kineret and their removal could threaten his ability to generate electricity. He rattled his sabre when he pointed to the concession he had from the Government for all Palestinian water relevant to electrification. He also had plans for a second generator in the Hula Valley and it mattered little that, later, this never came to fruition.

He worried too that, when the Peel Commission began work in 1937 in Palestine, there was talk of Partition that might place his Naharayim plant outside the Jewish part of Palestine and hence out of his control. But in the end, his interventions were far from the only reason why the Hula was not fully drained until after the State of Israel was formed. Expense and internal squabbles amongst the Zionists were more relevant causes for the delay.

Rutenberg's counter-proposal for settlement on land on the other side of the Jordan River now became a major focus of his attention. He had formed an interesting friendship with the Emir Abdullah of Jordan and was hopeful that he might gain his support for a peace-initiative he was hatching. Discussions over the years had centred on the prospect of financial and other aid for Jordan in exchange for access to land east of the river for Jews and for displaced Palestinian Arabs. It is the case too that Jabotinsky and the Revisionists had always believed that Trans-Jordan should be part of the Mandatory territories into which the Jews had a right to immigrate. Rutenberg and Jabotinsky were as one on this, and on many other views, about the future of Israel. They formed the basis of a firm friendship. At the end of 1930 there were offers by Jordanian Sheiks to sell 30,000 dunam of land to the Jews. They proposed that the land could be used for 'joint economic activities', a suggestion that was close to Rutenberg's heart.

By mid 1932, Abdullah himself was offering to lease 70,000 dunam to Jewish institutions with a six months' option on a 99 year lease for £2,000 per month. An agreement was reached in January 1933 but then it all fell by the wayside. Sadly, while the Nashashibis supported the deal, the Husseinis objected vehemently. The High Commissioner and Colonial Office were concerned that the Arabs of Palestine led by Haj Amin al-Husseini would never tolerate the idea, and Philby in Jordan was warning of opposition there too. Rutenberg had by now become painfully aware that Abdullah was a minor figure in the Middle East political arena. Poor and isolated, Abdullah was feeling the heat and decided to quietly withdraw.

Rutenberg was frustrated yet again but his pursuit of Arab-Jewish peace, at least on his terms, was relentless. He understood before many that for a long-term solution to the conflict much more needed to be done to understand the Arab viewpoint. They were being pushed out of their land by the Jews and any solution would require Jewish concessions.

By 1936 he was once more joining forces with Judah Magnes, the prominent but deeply unpopular pursuer of peace at any cost. They, together with a peculiarly matched team of individuals formed a morally upright group of five individuals, 'The Five', including David Fromkin, Moshe Novomeysky and Moshe Smilansky, non-political but peacefully minded figures, sadly with little influence.

Only Rutenberg had much political experience, while the others, although highly intelligent and respected, were politically naïve. Rutenberg was not entirely free of rose-tinted spectacles either.

He took a while to accept that bribery did not always work and he was forced to recognise that the old guard of corrupt Arab leadership had been usurped by young more idealistic nationalists who were immune to bribes. Just as there were disputes within the Jewish camp, there were warring factions within the Arab camp too. The young Arabs were certainly more aggressive and frequently resorted to threats and bloodshed.

'The Five' went ahead and developed a peace plan, most of which resembled Rutenberg's original proposals that he had presented to the Colonial Secretary, Passfield, in 1930. It included two separately elected Governing bodies, one for the Arabs and one for the Jews, with an overarching Mandatory body for disputed matters and for foreign affairs and the like. He wrote to the Chairman of his Electric Company, now Lord Samuel, that, since Balfour's Declaration, 'we Jews have done nothing to deal with the moral and psychological aspects of the fact that we are coming to a land which Arabs have serious national claims of ownership over. The Arabs have a new young, population which cannot be bribed. They are educated, enlightened and proud, with some culture and much courage.'

He then proposed that Jewish immigration should be limited to 30,000 per annum for 10 years, at the end of which time there would be 800,000 Jews making up 40% of the population. He went so far as to specify the type of Jews who should be allowed to immigrate, the young and fit, and those with enough capital.

He found at least two leading Arab figures who seemed interested. Musa al'Alami, legal council to the British

Administration, and Musa al'Khalidi, but neither of them were representative of the Arab leadership. Rutenberg had tried to get the agreement of Moshe Shertock (later renamed Sharett) who became Israel's second Prime Minister, and Menachem Ushisskin (past head of the Zionist Commission) in the Jewish Agency with little support from them either.

Even his good friend Berl Katznelson tried to point out the impracticability of his ideas. Although the High Commissioner expressed modest support, it was becoming clear to Rutenberg that neither the Arabs nor the Jews were convinced of his proposals.

Of course, that was not the end of his efforts. Characteristically he believed he was hampered by his four colleagues, particularly Magnes who was persona non grata within the Yishuv. He decided to continue alone with his customary secretive negotiations. Unfortunately for him he was no more successful with those than he had been with 'The Five'.

The problems were obvious, if not to him then to most of the parties that he needed to convince. The Arabs, under Husseini and increasingly dominated by young Arabs, wanted nothing to do with any Jewish immigration at all and certainly no sale of land to the Jews. Bribery no longer worked if ever it had done. On the Jewish side, the leadership were less than enthusiastic about limiting immigration in the way he proposed. Ben Gurion was not entirely averse but was sufficiently circumspect about putting a number to immigration. He understood how controversial it might be. Rutenberg had long discussions with High Commissioner

Wauchope, in which he strongly reiterated his pressure for the Administration to beef up its policing and troop numbers and to take a firm hand with the striking Arabs. Wauchope had always been keen to see reconciliation between Arab and Jew but by now any 'peace plan' was being overtaken by the 1937 Peel Commission's Inquiry into the unstable conditions in Palestine. Wauchope was unwilling to go out on a limb while the Inquiry was in progress.

This was the time when the idea of Partition was in the air and Rutenberg began to rethink his priorities.

CHAPTER 22

A last gasp venture into politics

By 1936 Rutenberg was entering the last six years of his life and his health was marred by an increasing toll of illness, not that he spent much time revealing it to anyone nor did he complain. Frustrated, Rutenberg was impatiently pacing around his empty house in Haifa, still full of grand ideas and striving to achieve great things. But less notice was beginning to be taken of his views within British Departments of Government. A loose cannon, still firing off impractical ideas, was the view around Parliament. His proposals to split the Arabs by coming down hard on those who were hostile while dealing kindly with those who were willing to collaborate had not found favour with the High Commissioner, the Colonial Office or the Jewish Agency. Nor, of course, amongst the Arabs. And his idea that a deal with Abdullah in Jordan would provide an answer to the question of land in which to settle, was doomed by the clamour of the Palestinian Arabs.

Nevertheless, he retained the respect and admiration of the Yishuv of Palestine and, as we will see, by 1939 he was being pressed to take on the leadership of the Va'ad HaLeumi once more.

By then the Yishuv was in complete disarray with in-fighting between the Histradut (the powerful Trade Union movement) and the right wing revisionists, and between the Jewish Agency on the one hand and the Va'ad HaLeumi on the other. Powerful personalities dominated the often violent disagreements between and within these organizations. Ben Gurion and Berl Katznelson were bastions of the left while Jabotinsky led from the right. He, however, was of less influence within Palestine after his expulsion by the High Commissioner in 1929. Somewhere near the middle were Weizmann, Sokoloff and Ussishkin. Rutenberg was at the centre amongst the various factions with his calls for unity.

It was obvious to him and many others that the years between 1936 and 1939 were increasingly serious for the future of the Jewish State. The Arabs were extremely active in violent uprisings in Palestine and very effective vocally in marshalling support in Britain, both in Parliament and in Government. The need for unity amongst the warring Jewish groups was desperate and Rutenberg was soon to bring all his strength to try to achieve it. It was his, and the Jews, misfortune that he was ultimately unsuccessful.

The Government was casting around for solutions to the dilemmas they faced in trying to get out of the quagmire of the Arab-Jewish battle. By now it was a war. They were losing heart when, in 1937, they set up yet another Commission of Inquiry, this time led by Lord Peel. It was a series of severe strikes by the Arabs against both the Administration and the Jews that was making life difficult for the British Government. Between 1936 and 1938 strikes were accompanied by murder and mayhem, and only the imposition of martial law belatedly brought some relief. The heavy troop pressure had been something Rutenberg had been seeking for many years but Britain hardly needed this distraction when India was pressing for independence and Hitler's Germany was making a European war increasingly likely. Rutenberg calculated that it was inevitable that Britain would want to placate the Arabs, if only to keep the Muslims of India on side.

Riots and strikes continued throughout 1936 until an uneasy truce allowed Earl Peel to embark on his Inquiry.

His report of 1937 clearly recognised that the Arab and Jewish communities could never co-exist in Palestine. He exposed the defect in Balfour's Declaration, concluding that it was impossible to establish a homeland for Jews in Palestine while at the same time protecting the civil and religious rights of the Arabs living on the same piece of land. It had always been a hopeless proposition. Both sides would have had to compromise but there had never been any sign that a compromise acceptable to both parties had been feasible. The only solution, said Peel, was a division of the land – partition – with separate Arab and Jewish states.

Partition had been muted before, but now it was put forward for consideration by a British Government under pressure to sort out Palestine once and for all.

Partition worried Rutenberg. He, who was nothing if not an expansionist, could see that a diminution in the size of the Jewish land would limit the need for his electricity and, if Naharayim finished up in the proposed Arab state, he would lose control of his precious power plant.

Peel's tentative partition plan was complex and involved an area of land to be retained by the Mandatory Authority that split and diminished both Arab and Jewish putative states (*Diagram 6*). Even then it was recognised as unworkable, but the Government decided to have another go and the Woodhead Commission of Inquiry followed.

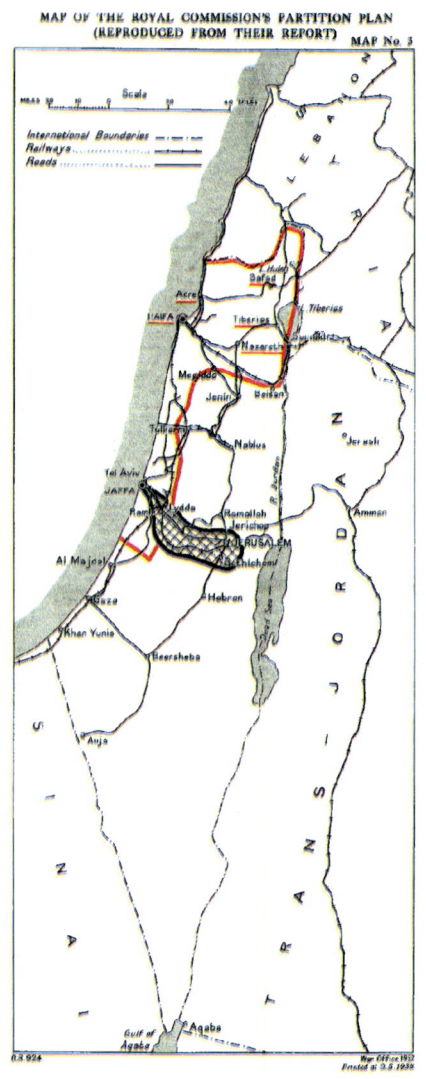

Diagram 6: Partition Plan, Peel Report

It was a farce. These Commissioners recommended three different options for partition with each member of the Inquiry favouring a different option. They just about managed to compromise and recommend one of the plans. Rutenberg need not have worried that his power plant on the Jordan would end up in an Arab state or under a separate Mandatory rule since each of the proposed partition plans was found to be unacceptable or unworkable by the Government. The Jewish Agency on the other hand was ready to accept partition – for the first time it gave them a State – and even if it was only the size of Norfolk, it was a start. The Arabs hated it for the same reason. The Government then found that partition was completely impractical. Too expensive and the Arabs would never wear it.

With war in Europe looming, the Government decided to knock heads together by convening a conference in London to be attended by Arab and Jewish representatives and, if the parties could not agree, the Government would impose their own solution.

This was a serious threat and threw the Jewish leadership into disarray. They failed to agree on how to respond to the prospect of an imposed solution.

Rutenberg's initial reaction was to be incensed. He told everyone who would listen that they must boycott the London Conference. No good would come out of it. The Jews will lose as the Arabs are given everything they want. He knew how the Government thought and that they were now thoroughly fed up with the Jews. What he hoped to achieve by this is unclear although he was not alone in his view.

Soon, however, he changed his opinion quite radically.

Weizmann, on the other hand, reluctantly agreed to attend.

It is not too difficult to understand the dilemma. Should the Zionists go along with Britain despite the treatment that was threatened or fight against the Government when they knew that they had to support its efforts against the much larger threat posed by Germany? That they could not afford to alienate

Britain when they were about to fight a much bigger enemy was a bitter pill for the Jews to swallow. Some, like Jabotinsky, were ambivalent, but Rutenberg was eventually able to accept the Government's proposal despite his initial aversion.

CHAPTER 23

1939, threat of war and the 'White Paper'

The London meeting was by no means straight-forward. The Arab representatives were divided into two warring camps and, at first, they would not sit down together. The Husseini camp had been in a vicious war with the Nashashibi camp for some time. Mayhem and slaughter were common features. A truce of sorts was prompted by the Colonial Office Minister, Malcolm MacDonald, who threatened to negotiate separately with each clan. Although the Palestinians were led by Jamal Husseini, they answered to the ex-Mufti, Haj Amin al Husseini, exiled from Palestine for his role in anti-British violence and now holed up in Beirut. On the other hand, Britain regarded Ibn Saud in Saudi Arabia as being more significant and someone they needed to keep on side to protect British strategic interests in the event of war. The Jews too were divided with Weizmann and the Zionist Organisation in attendance while Rutenberg and the Va'ad HaLeumi shunning the meeting. That did not stop Rutenberg sitting in the side lines in London, increasingly worried and frustrated.

He did, however, demonstrate his skill as a mediator between disputatious antagonists whom he knew were spoiling the Jewish case. He had already shown his capacity to bring

Trade Union movements together when they argued amongst themselves in the 1920s.

Ben Gurion was beginning to take over the mantle of Jewish leadership from Weizmann, something that was already divisive. A split between Jabotinsky and Ben Gurion was yet another disastrous division. Ben Gurion, on the left, could not abide Jabotinsky, on the right, likening him to Hitler for the way in which he had been rabble rousing against the Arabs and the Mandate. Rutenberg, recognising that the squabbling within the Jewish camps was damaging their position with the Government, faced the challenge of bringing Ben Gurion and Jabotinsky together. This he managed to achieve even though the truce, when it occurred, was but temporary.

Rutenberg had been Jabotinsky's friend from the time in 1914 when they worked together in their struggle to form a Jewish Brigade to fight with Britain, and later when they fought side by side against the rioting Arabs in 1921. Ben Gurion was facing the dilemma of whether to go along with Jabotinsky's ideas for an armed revolt or take a more moderate approach? He was now desperate and bereft of ideas and threatened to resign.

Meanwhile the focus of attention was on the London Conference. The Arab and Jewish contingents sat in separate rooms, left by different doors and never met. MacDonald and his Prime Minister, Neville Chamberlain, gave the same addresses to both groups separately. It soon became clear that the Jews would come out worse. Rutenberg's bribes had failed, his efforts to split more moderate Arabs from the more extreme elements did not bear fruit and the Government had only belatedly been able to control any of the riots and strikes.

The Government and the Arabs had rejected partition and now, with the war in Europe about to begin, the only way forward, as a matter of urgency, was for MacDonald to impose a solution. It was always going to favour the Arabs, especially as Britain hoped to keep the huge Muslim population of India on side. They already had hopes that the Indians would fight with the British if war was declared.

The essence of the Government's 'White Paper' that emerged was a severe limitation on land purchase by Jews and a marked restriction on immigration for ten years, at the end of which time the population at large (namely the majority Arab population) would determine whether further immigration would be allowed. It seemed like the end of the Jewish dream of a homeland of their own. It was particularly hard to take when the Jews of Germany, who were being herded up and sent to concentration camps, needed a country where they might be welcome. Palestine was almost unique in that regard.

It was borne in on the Jews that armed Arab uprisings had been much more effective than their own efforts towards a negotiated solution.

It now seemed that all Weizmann's wooing of British Ministers would be in vain as the Government's 'White Paper', published on 17th of May, 1939, kicked him in the face. Rutenberg was incensed but could do little to lessen the blow.

Weizmann resigned and Rutenberg returned to an increasingly apprehensive Yishuv in Palestine.

CHAPTER 24

Struggle for unity

In retrospect it is hardly surprising that the Yishuv turned again to Rutenberg for leadership. The Jews of Palestine were devastated when the 'White Paper' was published in May. It was obvious to them that they had fallen into a trap.

Anger and frustration spilt over into violent demonstrations by the Jews against the British Government and its Administration. The White Paper was seen for what it was, a complete betrayal and a severe blow to Zionism. And the Jewish leadership bore the brunt of the inflamed criticism on the street. Weizmann, with his pro-British stance, was regarded with derision for failing to prevent the outcome of the London Conference. The fact that he was powerless in the face of the Government's determination meant little within the Yishuv.

Ben Gurion came in for particular criticism too. Questions were being asked. Where was the plan of action? If there was a plan, what was it? Why was nothing happening? And, where was the leadership?

This was the moment when the division of opinion between the Jewish Agency and the Yishuv widened even more. Rutenberg was not shy of criticising the Jewish Agency as being unrepresentative and out of touch. Ben Gurion, on the other hand felt that the Va'ad HaLeumi was interested only in Palestinian Jews and was ignoring the plight of those in the diaspora. Squaring the circle had become almost impossible.

Who or what should now lead was hotly disputed.

Naturally Rutenberg's name kept coming up. Widely admired for what he had achieved and his lack of allegiance to any political party made him an attractive proposition. He seemed just the sort of leader the Yishuv wanted in such threatening times when the need for action was urgent. Democratic principles could be cast aside when decisive action was required. Rutenberg fitted the bill as leader, just as Britain, in her time of need, turned to Winston Churchill despite his chequered history, at almost the same time.

Rutenberg's qualifications for leadership were impressive. As a successful entrepreneur he had provided employment for a very large workforce. He was liked by the socialists as one of their own, and by the capitalists for his business acumen and success. Both were able to overlook his dictatorial propensities and anti-democratic attitudes. In the emergency that they faced, they needed a 'strong man of action'.

And he had shown considerable skills in his efforts to bring together Jewish warring parties, who were forever at each other's throats. Witness his efforts to get Jabotinsky and Ben Gurion to meet and agree, if only for a short while, and to encourage Jabotinsky and the left-wing Ben Zvi of the Va'ad HaLeumi, to reach an agreement. He had also been successful in helping resolve a labour dispute between rival trade unions, the HaHistradut Haleumit (Federation of Workers in Tel Aviv) and Histradut Haclalit (General Federation of Labour).

And when the long running dispute erupted between the underground armed forces, the Haganah allied to the Mapai Party of Ben Gurion, and Etzel, the right wing force that used more overt violence against the British Administration, Rutenberg was involved in trying to bring an easing of their differences.

He was perceived as having a further advantage in his relatively easy access to the High Commissioner and to significant political figures in the British Government. His friendly contacts with a number of Arab leaders were seen as extra assets. Ben Gurion reluctantly admired him while constantly pointing to his political naïvety.

It was not too unexpected that the Yishuv would turn once again to him for leadership although it was unfortunate that there was only limited recognition within Palestine that Rutenberg's star was waning in the eyes of the British Government.

Within three days of his appointment, Rutenberg held a press conference. He, who had abhorred publicity, had probably decided to set out his plans early so that he could have a free hand thereafter without having to obtain agreement from anyone. In his presentation he concentrated on the need for unity amongst the Jews if they were going to be able to deal with Britain and its 'White Paper'. They would not be able to persuade the British Government or the Administration in Palestine to help them if they were constantly battling amongst themselves.

He moved on to the parlous state of the economy that had been exacerbated by the 40,000 unemployed. He would press the Government for a grant or a loan, but the Jews would also have to think about how they could help themselves. He came up with the unpopular idea of taxation; a system in which everyone earning a wage would contribute according to their income. It was not a unique idea but it was certainly an unusual proposal in the Middle East unused to the idea of paying tax. Hardly a surprise that it was hotly resisted immediately by the workers and soon watered down.

It was his misfortune too, that two efforts to form a united group amongst the Jewish leadership were unsuccessful.

The first, in June 1939, was the formation of a 'Council of Five'. It included Rutenberg of the Va'ad HaLeumi as Chairman, Berl Katznelson of the Histradut trade union, David Remez, the leader of the Mapai Party, Rav Gold of Hamisrachi and Israel Rokach on the right. It was hardly surprising that such a determined group of individualists could barely agree on anything.

The next effort was to form a 'Triumvirate' made up of the leaders of the Jewish Agency Executive, the Zionist Executive Council and the Va'ad HaLeumi. Not much chance there either of agreement amongst strong minded and independent Jews.

It was Ben Gurion who suggested that the Jews should fight the 'White Paper' as if there was no war and fight the war as if there was no 'White Paper'. It was an almost impossible proposition to achieve and Rutenberg knew it. He would not last long as leader in 1939, but the war years made it difficult for anyone to remain in a safe position. Yet Rutenberg worked tirelessly to try to make the best of the almost unacceptable pack of cards the Jews had been dealt.

Having been vociferous in his objection to any Jewish attendance at the London Conference, he now turned around completely in his efforts to collaborate with Britain.

He concentrated on the art of the possible. What were the areas where some form of agreement could be reached despite the strictures on immigration and land purchase? Where was the room for manoeuvre within the Government's firmly held rules? Economic development and industrialisation were the topics on which he concentrated, making the case that these were certainly in Britain's interests in their war effort. Always a man of vision, he believed that helping Britain during the war now would stand them in good stead when they tried to revoke the 'White Paper' after the war. He had come to the firm conclusion that his efforts should be focussed on the development of Palestine for the Jews since there was little he could do for the ill-fated Jews of Europe.

Ben Gurion thought he was not only naïve in taking this line but accused him of being motivated more by his own business interests than for the good of the country. Of course, Rutenberg denied allegations of self-interest even though he was heavily engaged in Electricity Company business at the same time and was laying further claims for funds at the Government's door.

1940 saw him in London again with a full hand of bids. He had gained some support from High Commissioner, Sir Harold MacMichael, before he left. He made several of his proposals to Lord Lloyd, Secretary of State at the Colonial Office, and then made an outrageous suggestion to Sir Robert Bruce-Lockhart as we will see.

He first returned to his argument that the Arabs were not of one mind and could be split. A mixture of bribes for the more moderate Arab leaders, like the Nashashibis, and a much firmer hand against the activists in the Husseini camp, would help resolve the differences between Arab and Jew. He had been propounding this idea for some years and had repeatedly had cold water thrown on it by the officials and by Ben Gurion. Those Arabs that Rutenberg relied upon to intercede on behalf of the Jews, Emir Abdullah, the Nashashibis and Nuri Said of Iraq, clearly lacked any power against the Grand Mufti. He took time to recognise their limitations.

Then he sought approval to bring in refugee immigrants to help fight with the British. He wanted able-bodied European refugees who had capital to invest, to be given permission to emigrate to Palestine. He had started earlier, when he met General Lord Gort in Palestine, with a high bid for a quota of 100,000 refugees to bolster the defence of the country. The number was slowly whittled down to 2,000 when he spoke to High commissioner MacMichael, and by the time he met Lord Lloyd in London he was bidding for 300 out of the quota allowed for the Jewish Agency. They should come from amongst the German Jews who had escaped Hitler and were now in hiding in Holland and Switzerland. This was a fine group of men and women ready and willing to fight against the Fascist scourge at Britain's side. Sir John Shuckburgh was sympathetic. He said that as usual Rutenberg had excellent ideas but lacked the support of the Jewish Agency. He would certainly need their approval. He insisted that these immigrants would have to come out of their overall allocation.

Pinchas hid his bid from the Jewish Agency Executive and when they heard of it, they objected strongly. Once again, he was undermined by his fellow Jews.

Despite his demands for immigrants shrinking dramatically he was ultimately disappointed.

His next request was for economic help to develop industry in Palestine. He needed a grant of £5 million to build up the infrastructure, roads, railways and electricity that would be invaluable for Britain in such a strategically important part of the world. What Colonial Office officials saw were not valuable assets in their war effort but an attempt by an upstart Jew to gain economic advantages over the Arabs.

Thomas Bennett, of the Colonial office, followed the prevailing anti-Semitic view within the Department and was dead set against Rutenberg. He advised accordingly: 'Minister, you cannot seriously be considering investing in building up the land for the Israelites in the face of the 'White Paper' that specifically precludes that idea?' Despite the advice, Lloyd was sympathetic, at least temporarily. Unhappily for Rutenberg by this time he was increasingly being looked upon as a spent force who could be safely ignored.

And ignore him they did when he sought a separate £1 million for Jordanian developments that he was trying to mastermind with the Emir Abdullah. Finally, his offer to travel to America to raise arms for a Jewish fighting force to support the British war effort was turned down. He was far from the man the Government needed to make this case when they were trying to get arms from America for themselves. If he wanted to go to the USA on his own behalf they would not stand in the way of him approaching the Foreign Office. A typically ambivalent and cool response by a distracted Government more reliant on the Jewish Agency for any communication. By now he was completely disillusioned.

The most he got out of all these approaches was permission by the High Commissioner, Sir Harold MacMichael, to include immigrants with sufficient capital in the list of those to be allowed into Palestine under the aegis of the Jewish Agency. Not a great victory.

There was one other meeting he had in London, this time with Sir Robert Bruce-Lockhart (*Fig. 34*).

This was to be a last flourish of Rutenberg's characteristically bold and unconventional ideas. He had met Bruce-Lockhart in St. Petersburg in 1917 when he had been the British Vice Consul. It was there that he took him to one side and quietly discussed the prospect of Lenin and Trotsky being done away with. Bolshevism was a clear and obvious danger, not only to Russia but to Britain, Europe and the rest of the free world. Would he help in their assassination?

Figure 34: Sir Robert Bruce-Lockhart

After all it would be in Britain's best interests. It was just a little outside Bruce-Lockhart's remit and he declined the invitation. Remarkably he later became the British envoy to the Bolshevik Government and it was in that position that he developed as a significant spy whose auto-biography was a sensation in the 1930s. Paradoxically, he was arrested for allegedly plotting to assassinate Lenin. Imprisoned for a while, he was later released in exchange for a Soviet spy. Rutenberg knew that he had form when he caught up with him again in London in 1939, this time with another assassination proposal. Haj Amin al Husseini was a serious danger to Britain and to the Jews of Palestine. He was in league with Hitler and had been plotting the overthrow of the British Mandate for years. Would he help get rid of him once and for all? They could save tens of thousands of lives by killing one evil man. Would he approach the Government? Clearly he could not say anything about Rutenberg being involved in this proposal.

Bruce-Lockhart was not entirely surprised. Why else would Pinchas seek him out after all these years?

He responded cautiously. He knew what Rutenberg was capable of and recognised that he was serious.

He decided to float the idea tentatively with the Colonial Secretary.

 Sorely tempted, after all Husseini was no friend of Britain, Lloyd nevertheless vetoed the idea. Politically toxic and difficult to achieve with Husseini now ensconced in Germany. Likely to be too messy and embarrassing, it was a nice idea, but there was no way the government could condone it.

Pinchas had another remarkable, if entirely logical, proposal for Bruce-Lockhart. It had significant implications for Britain but, sadly, was badly timed. Russia had recently signed the Molotov-Ribbentrop Pact that kept them out of the war against Germany but Rutenberg recognised that the pact would not last. He proposed that Britain should make every effort to woo the Stalin Government round to the Allies side. He put forward his usual mixture of Machiavellian ideas. Bribery first. Britain should offer financial incentives to the Russians. Secondly, they should place a British Ambassador in St. Petersburg, and thirdly they should set up a network of spies in Russia to promote relationships with Britain. He even produced a list of names from amongst his old revolutionary friends who would make excellent spies. Kerensky, Vishinik and Zanazinov would do a great job.

When this idea was relayed to the Foreign Office it was, of course, derided. There was some surreptitious interest in the idea of a spy network. After all, Communism was abhorrent to the Government. But Rutenberg's old friends were clearly passe as agents and that idea was rejected out of hand. This was one of Pinchas's typically far-sighted ideas that, if adopted early enough, might have shortened the war. It certainly demonstrated his continuing interest in events in Russia, but once again, good as they might have been, his suggestions were lost.

By now there was certainly a strong undercurrent of personal antipathy to Rutenberg within Whitehall, and his ideas were simply regarded as more of his wild speculations that Ministers could safely ignore.

Finally, he met with the Management Committee of his Electricity Company to deal with some of its business, all rather secret. As was his usual practice, only when he returned to Palestine did he reveal to the Executive of the Va'ad HaLeumi what he had been up to in London.

CHAPTER 25

Ill health catches up

Once again by 1941 he was back in Palestine, disillusioned and about to resign from the leadership of the Va'ad HaLeumi. He was casting around for enemies amongst the Jews whom he could blame in the resignation speech he gave at the King David Hotel in Jerusalem. It was vindictive and no-one escaped his criticism. He was certainly correct in pointing to the splintering of Jewish organisations and to the constant argument and in-fighting. Not much new there in Jewish politics. In vain did he continue to urge a greater unity of purpose.

He saved some of his most pointed criticism for the Histradut, the Trade Union movement headed by his friend Berl Katznelson. Always a socialist but never a democrat, Rutenberg controlled his own huge workforce and prevented them joining the Histradut. Now he was at their throat. To him, they were splitting Jewish society with their aggressive methods. Violent and threatening behaviour within their own groups was making it impossible to make the Yishuv a united force to face the British Government. When the need was for the Jews to exert what little influence they had, the British could sit back and watch the Jews destroy themselves.

He then turned on the Jewish Agency. While he had some sympathy for the lot of the workers he had none at all for the

Jewish Agency. Too far out of touch with the man in the street. Too much involved in international politics to recognise the needs of the Yishuv. How can they possibly hope to represent them when they had so little idea of their feelings, or for that matter, of the Arabs.

And for the Va'ad HaLeumi whose leadership he had just relinquished he said, they were wasting so much time on elections and a quest for representation – internal politics – instead of focussing on what was desperately needed, a search for investment and enterprise to build up agriculture and industry. He had no time for representative democracy. He wanted action not what he perceived as floundering around with the internal affairs of the Va'ad HaLeumi.

Figure 35: Berl Katznelson, Head of Trade Union, Histradut, and an intellectual founder of Israel

He did not mention anyone by name but it was clear that he had Ben Gurion and his friend Berl Katznelson in his sights.

The reaction to his speech was immediate. He received large numbers of supportive letters and messages from the Yishuv. His words resonated with the man and woman in the street, especially the young. But he was not surprised that the leaders of each of his targets reacted bitterly. He was undisturbed by them except when his friend Katznelson thoroughly destroyed his arguments (*Fig. 35*). He was deeply hurt by Berl's carefully considered response in which he criticised his undemocratic ways, and his dismissal of anyone who tried to limit his actions. His recourse to 'the opinion of the masses' had already led him to be likened to Hitler by Foreign Office officials, and to Mussolini by Ben Gurion.

By now he was seriously ill, locked away in his house in Haifa and hardly talking to anyone. Certainly not speaking in public, it is uncertain whether he could even do so when he was suffering from what was likely to be a cancer in his throat.

A sad end of so vital a man with a huge personality.

CHAPTER 26

A hero's demise

There are few heroes in Israeli history who are not free from controversy and Pinchas Rutenberg was certainly not one of them.

But there is little doubt that he figures highly amongst the many outstanding figures responsible for Israel's foundations.

His was a life of many contradictions. He started out as a socialist revolutionary in Russia and was certainly involved in a messy assassination. Yet he ended up as a wealthy entrepreneur industrialist in Palestine. Heavily involved in negotiations between Arabs and Jews and having a high public persona, he kept his private life hidden. This is the man who through sheer force of personality had been able to influence many of the most significant and leading figures in Russia, in the UK and in Palestine. The range of his activities is remarkable even in an age of remarkable men.

He mixed closely with the hierarchy in the British Administration in Palestine, the Government in London and leading Zionists in America and Britain. He was firm friends with Maxim Gorky, had more than a passing relationship with Benito Mussolini in Italy and was on close personal terms with the Emir Abdullah of Trans-Jordan. He was involved in the setting up of the American Jewish Congress, in the start of Haganah (Jewish Defence Force) and in developing the Palestine Airways, quite apart from assuming the leadership of the Jewish representative body for the Yishuv, the Va'ad HaLeumi. And all the while twisting arms and using his capacity for persuasion to gain the concession to electrify Palestine – his most lasting contribution to the future state of Israel. Yet despite his powerful public persona he kept his own life very much to himself.

Some regarded him as the devil incarnate, responsible for assassinations and revolutionary activities; a man almost impossible to control. Others thought of him as a man devoted to the Jewish homeland who not only brought the electricity to Palestine that fostered its future progress, but worked hard for co-operation between Arabs and Jews.

His driving ideology was difficult to pin down as he retained a strong socialist bent on the one hand and a keen eye for business on the other. A friend of poets, writers and rabbis, at the forefront for equality for Arabs but at the same time dictatorial, domineering and downright awkward, little wonder he was so difficult to classify.

Hardly surprising then, that a man of such strong character and so difficult to characterise, irritated so many in the British Government, amongst the Zionists and within the Arab communities as he drove ahead with his ideas and with little restraint.

An extremely talented engineer with unbounded energy and a great talent for organisation, it was almost entirely due to his efforts that Palestine received the electricity it desperately needed for its agricultural and industrial development. And he was able to see his plans through to success because of his matching capacity for business and entrepreneurship. He not only masterminded the plans for the electrification schemes, both hydro and diesel powered, he convinced a sceptical, and often hostile, British Parliament to grant him the concession to do so. And he had to persuade a Zionist Organisation that was far from fully supportive.

But it was not merely electricity he supplied. Indeed, views were beginning to be expressed in the Colonial Office and amongst the Zionists, that there was no need for his massive hydro-electric generator on the Jordan River. Weizmann thought that they could make do with just a few diesel plants around the country. But all that ignored the rather more important bonuses that came from building the plant on the Jordan. It provided employment for several thousand workmen at a time when unemployment in the country was running high. It encouraged immigration when it was beginning to lapse. And it created a huge financial influx from foreign investors when there was little else to attract outside funding.

But there is a problem in trying to separate his ability to achieve great things on the ground from his characteristic bombast, bluntness, and serious capacity to irritate so many. Against all his achievements we have to set the difficulties posed by these abrasive characteristics. It is entirely conceivable, of course, that he would not have been successful without them. Perhaps they were interdependent?

However, we can ask how did someone succeed when he rejected the very idea of representative democracy, when he could not bear to be constrained by a need to consult committees or boards of which he was sometimes the head, and when he gave away little information to those to whom he was ostensibly responsible? It is true, however, that he was very clever, highly intelligent and worked very hard in preparing his arguments. Yet he may never have learnt that what were appropriate tactics in business dealings were quite inappropriate in the soft-footed corridors of Whitehall. At no time could it be said of him that he was 'diplomatic'. Perhaps he compensated for this by his frightening and overbearing manner that few felt strong enough to oppose; at least in his first few years.

He was certainly an imposing figure, 'with a head like granite', who spoke through clenched teeth. The impression he made within aloof and superficially civilised Government circles must have been startling. Officials did not take to him. A man with blunt manners was never going to be liked. Nevertheless, he was not someone whom they could safely ignore, particularly as he had the ear of Churchill and other senior figures. Besides, he had some very good ideas. So, they swallowed hard and listened carefully before finally acceding to his requests. And he was able to overcome much opposition that would have deterred a lesser man in his plans for electrification of Palestine.

It could not last and his direct and often overbearing behaviour eventually undermined the confidence in which he had been reluctantly held. In the last few years of his life the view amongst

Government officials was one of ill-concealed contempt and he became a sad figure whom they could safely ignore.

He freely admitted that politics were beyond him. Ben Gurion labelled him politically naïve. He abhorred the very idea of 'politics' and spoke of 'politicians' with venom in his voice. 'Action' was what he craved and even when he accepted a leadership position in the Va'ad HaLeumi, he did it under his own conditions, in which democracy was little in evidence. He chose his small executive committee, selected local leaders around the country and ensured that the press were kept well out of his affairs. And he ignored his committee in his dealings in London, scarcely keeping them informed even after he returned.

From where did his anti-democratic stance derive? It is not difficult to see how his formative years in Russia must have played their part. As a revolutionary he became used to the idea of immediate and dramatic action without consulting the peasants or workers. Democracy was in abeyance as he and the intelligentsia knew what was best for the proletariat in the emergency they perceived was constantly in the air. And in Palestine Rutenberg continued to behave as if everything was urgent. It was the constant sense of urgency that permeated his every action that allowed him to take liberties with representative democracy. He knew exactly what he wanted to do although he was fully capable of pragmatic swerves when the need arose. As any good businessman, he knew how to make deals. When it became clear that he was not going to make headway in gaining a concession to supply electricity to Trans-Jordan he backed down to fight another day. And when the flow in the Auja (Yarkon) River was shown to be far too trivial to be capable of generating electricity, he rapidly changed his plans to diesel sources. And furthermore, he not only convinced the British Government that this was in their best interests, he also bamboozled them into allowing him to buy his equipment from Germany, where it was much cheaper than in Britain. He was certainly capable of bare-faced cheek or 'Chutzpah'.

However, it was when he ventured into the overtly political arena where he was found wanting and where he received the most criticism.

There were two occasions when he was asked to take on a political leadership role. Both were for the Va'ad HaLeumi, the representative body for the Yishuv – the Jewish general population of Palestine. Both ended in failure and he resigned within a year or so. Full of bright ideas he might have been, but his sense of what was practical or possible left him floundering. The Va'ad HaLeumi executive soon lost faith in him, Ben Gurion thought he was hopelessly lost in the art of political possibilities and Weizmann never forgave him for blundering into his delicate and protracted negotiations with Governments. The feeling was mutual. Rutenberg thought Weizmann was wasting his time in hapless internal wranglings in Zionist Congresses and the like and with international players. Instead, he should be focussing on raising funds to invest in building up the industrial and agricultural base of the State. Practical investment on the ground, as advocated by Louis Brandeis in America, was where he believed he should be focussing his efforts. That, and bringing the Arabs on board by supporting their aspirations along with those of the Jews, were his aims.

These two messages, investment in the future with funds and manpower plus support for the Arabs, underpinned Rutenberg's every action on the political front. And it was in just those areas where he unfortunately failed the most. It was unfortunate too for the future of a Jewish homeland. Over several years, he returned repeatedly to his bid for investment in a large sinking fund that could be used to develop the infrastructure of the future State. Neither the British Government nor private enterprise were willing to invest despite the validity of his case. He could not understand why the Government could not accept the wisdom of the ideas he put to them. It would be to their considerable advantage to have a successful, prosperous ally in the Middle East. They, on the other hand, saw only a grasping Jew who wanted to line his own nest. Ben Gurion too was suspicious, and Weizmann would not countenance the support of his despised colleague. The obvious commercial success of Rutenberg's Palestine Electric Company and his own personal wealth inevitably made the suspicions stick. His protests were in vain and it mattered little that his motives were purer than they gave him credit for.

He swam against the tide of Zionist opinion in his relationships with the Arabs. He recognised early that the Arab residents in Palestine could not be ignored. They too had rights to the land and the Jews would need to come to some arrangement with them. He was part of the peace movement with Judah Magnes and others and was friendly with many Arab leaders, not least the Emir Abdullah of Jordan. He kept returning to the idea that the British Government should do its best to bring moderate Arab leaders over to an agreement while clamping down hard on the rioting opposition. He believed the former could be persuaded, perhaps by bribes that he handed out freely, while the latter, the minority he felt, should be stamped on hard. This attitude brought him into further conflict with the Zionists but earned him respect from a series of High Commissioners and high Government officials. It allowed him access when others were denied it.

His dislike of publicity and the press was part of his mode of operation. Always keen to present his ideas in private, he worked behind closed doors with those whom he felt had the power to make changes. He thought he could achieve more by personal persuasion than in a flurry of publicity. This was the manner of a businessman but it created much suspicion amongst those whom he ostensibly represented. The Jewish Agency and the Zionist Executive were also irritated when he went behind their backs, especially when, as often as not, he cut across their own negotiations. So long as he stuck to his electricity business there was less room for argument. But when he ventured into political matters he had his fingers burnt. Colonial Office Ministers and officials always deferred to the 'proper channels' leaving him hurt and disappointed.

This increasingly became the case in the last two years of his life when he lost much of his influence with the Government.

He still had supporters within the Yishuv where many believed that he was the hero who could lead them in the fight against the disaster of the 1939 'White Paper'. But by then he had retired from the field, literally struck dumb by his illness, and overcome by lethargy and exhaustion, a lonely sad figure isolated in his Haifa mansion.

When he died, on January 4th, 1942, there was an outpouring of international appreciation that had been less evident during his life.

Buried on Mount Scopus, amongst the workers as he requested, 'in a modest place among modest Jews', the funeral took place after a snow-storm, limiting the numbers who attended. Even in his will written a few days before he died, he was still trying to heal the rifts in Jewry. 'The split in our people has always worked against us. …This war between brothers has led us to trouble and if we don't cease it will destroy us. Whether we like it or not we are in the same boat.'

He stipulated in his will that there should be no eulogies read for him. He specified that his brother's sons should be his executors and disburse his fortune to the charity he set up to support the practical education of the young. It was to his nephews he turned to say the prayers at his grave side.

His will was clear. He wanted no towns, villages or streets to be named after him. In this he was almost entirely successful. Two small streets inconspicuously bear his name, one in Ramat Gan and another in Netanya. A power station was built bearing his name in Ashkelon, but only some years after he had died. All his money and possessions he left to establish the Rutenberg Institute (*Fig. 36*). It sits in his original house in Haifa and, as he requested, it provides education about the land of Israel for the young, mostly from abroad.

The day that he died the country went into national mourning. All places of entertainment closed. Despite his wish for no fuss to be made of his dying, there were speeches and eulogies by numerous dignitaries. The Mayor of Tel Aviv spoke tearfully for most when he said, 'This is a tremendous loss to the country and Nation'.

The Chief Secretary of the Palestinian Government, James MacPherson, said, 'Today we mourn a great man'. The president of the Histradut, David Remez, praised him for 'capturing the imagination and awakening the responsibility among the Zionists'.

His friend, Moshe Smilansky, in an emotional obituary a few days later, described Pinchas as someone whose 'whole personality and his appearance amongst us was wrapped in secrecy and magic'. His plans were always much bigger than the reality of the outcomes. He dreamt very big but he was not just a dreamer. Despite the limitations, 'the electricity project was a revolutionary turning point in the history of the Yishuv'.

Figure 36: Rutenberg Institute in Haifa

And he spoke of his great personal affection for Pinchas. 'I loved Rutenberg from the first day I met him – a great engineer with the soul of a poet. He had a weakness for giving orders and because I loved him, I carried out his orders.'

Rutenberg was undoubtedly a difficult man with many defects in his complex character but Smilansky's words are undeniable. 'We have lost a truly great man, one of those few who are given to us once in a generation.'

Index

Abdullah, Emir of Jordan	18, 85, 148, 153, 155, 185-187, 189, 200-201, 205, 219-220, 228, 234
Abraham Accords	195
AEG	136
Agricultural development	15, 190
Air Ministry High Command	139
Al'Alami, Musa	202
Al Aqsa Mosque	168
Al Husseini, Haj Amin	155, 172, 190, 201, 211, 222
Al-Husseini, Musa Kassem	97
Al'Khalidi, Musa	203
Alexandrovich, Grand Duke Sergei	40
Allenby, Field Marshal Edmund	69
Allenby Street	16-17, 136
America	27, 49-52, 54, 59, 61-62, 65, 68, 70, 75, 88, 93, 102-104, 108, 121, 143, 170, 178, 180, 220, 228, 233
American 'Crash'	146
American Jewish Congress	60, 228
American Palestine Development Corporation	107
Amery, Leo	111, 149
Amman	148
Antisemitism	20, 123
Arabs	12, 69, 72, 76, 81-84, 86, 90, 97-101, 116-117, 119, 123, 125-126, 129, 131-132, 136-137, 147-148, 166, 172, 174-178, 181, 183, 185-189, 192, 194, 197, 200-207, 209, 212-213, 219-220, 226, 228-229, 233-234

As salt	148
Ashkelon	236
Assassin	11, 19, 25
Assassination	20, 34-35, 39-40, 42-43, 70, 122, 221-222, 228
Assembly of Russian Factory and Mill Workers of St. Petersburg	29
Auja River (Yarkon River)	101, 109, 129-131, 133, 137
Azef, Yavno	24-25, 36-42
Bahrain	195
Balfour, Arthur	159, 178
Balfour Declaration	48, 57-58, 72, 74-76, 83, 86, 97, 99, 115-116, 121, 142, 147, 159, 177-178, 191, 193, 202, 207
Balfour-Beatty	165
Bank Hapoalim	109
Baron, Bernard	110
Bedouin	148
Beirut	198-199, 211
Ben Ami, Pinchas	53
Ben Gurion, David	191-192, 203, 206, 212, 214-219, 226-227, 232-234
Ben Zvi	215
Bennett, Thomas	220
Betar	50
Bevin, Ernest	193
'Big Four'	74-75
'Black Letter'	194
Bloody Sunday	33, 35
Blum, Leon	178
Blumgarten, Solomon (Yehoash)	15
Bols, General Sir Louis Jean	77
Bolshevik	11, 64-65, 117-118, 143, 185, 222
Brandeis, Louis	53, 59-60, 98, 102-104, 143, 233
Bribery	107, 172, 189, 195, 202-203, 223
Brindisi	50

British Air Ministry	198
British Parliament	19, 84, 230
Bruce-Lockhart, Sir Robert	218, 221-223
Buckmaster, Lord Stanley	122
Bundists	23, 56
Butcher, Sir John	124, 126
Cairo	81, 85
Capitalism and socialism	56
Cattle plague	147
Century Building	87
Chamberlain, Neville	212
Chancellor, Lt Colonel Sir John Robert	13, 116, 148, 168-169, 174-177, 179, 188-190, 192, 194, 197
Churchill, Winston	48, 78, 84-87, 98-99, 122, 125, 128, 130, 134-135, 149, 215, 231
Civil Administration	11, 83
Clausen, Gerard	91, 94
Clemenceau, Georges	36, 71-72, 74, 142
Colonial Office	77, 79, 84, 87-91, 94-95, 97, 99-100, 106-107, 110-111, 119, 122, 125, 128, 132-134, 139, 147-149, 157, 162, 168-169, 174-175, 177, 179-180, 183-184, 188-189, 192-193, 201, 205, 211, 218, 220, 230, 235
Concentration Camps	213
Concession for hydro-electrification	12, 17, 18, 29, 34, 42, 87, 89, 98, 100, 106, 115, 118-120, 122-127, 129, 131, 134, 138, 147-149, 159, 162-163, 166, 200, 229, 230, 232
Constantinople	66
Cossacks	33
Cox, Henry Fortnam	18, 153
Curzon, Lord George	90, 142
Dead Sea	77

Deputy Governor of Petrograd	63
De Haan, Jacob Israel	116
Diesel powered generators	139
Disputed borders	82
Dizengoff, Meir	136
Drummond-Shields, Sir Thomas	183
Dugdale, Blanche	159
Duma	63
Earthquakes	147
East End of London	37, 51, 193
Economic Federation	195
Einstein, Albert	178, 180
El Al	199
Entrepreneurship	19, 230
Eretz Yisroel	97
Etzel	216
Evening Standard	116
Executive Council	175, 217
Fascist	219
Feisal, Prince	72, 76, 81, 125
Fellahin	185, 187
Finland	25, 28, 37
Flender, Sir William	111-112
Foreign investors	19, 118, 230
Foreign Office	75, 84, 90, 110, 136, 141-142, 193, 221, 223, 227
France	37, 45, 47, 72, 75, 79-81, 142, 144
Frankfurter, Felix	60
Fraser and Chalmers	137
Fromkin, David	201
Fugitive	11
Fund-raising	59, 88, 91, 102, 118

Gallipoli	51
Gapon, Father Georgi	27-36, 38-41, 43, 127
General Electric Company	110
Geneva	35-36, 40, 83, 162
Gold, Rav	15, 217
Gorky, Maxim	33, 45-46, 65, 228
Gort, General Lord John	219
Grand Mufti	172, 182, 192, 219
Graves, Philip	117
Haganah	83, 216, 229
HaHashmal Street	17, 133
HaHistradut Haleumit	215
Haldane, Lord Richard	116
Hamisrachi	217
Hashomite	76, 85
Haycraft, Sir Thomas	83
Haycraft Report	83, 90
Hebrew	17, 59, 133, 157, 175, 178
Hebrew University	59, 175, 178
Hebron	172, 175
Henderson, Arthur	193
Herzl, Theodor	44
High Commissioner	11-13, 18, 73, 81, 83, 85, 88-90, 99, 109-110, 123-124, 131, 133, 147-149, 153-154, 168, 174, 176, 179, 185, 187, 189, 192, 194-195, 201, 203, 205-206, 216, 218-219, 221
Hirst, Sir Hugo	110
Histradut Haclalit	215
Holy Land	69
Homenko, Olga	27
Hope-Simpson, Sir John	183, 188-191
Hula Lake	199

Hula Valley	199-200
Hussein, King	76, 81-82
Husseini, Jamal	155, 172, 188, 190-192, 203, 211, 219, 222
Hydro-electricity	11, 18, 27, 49, 60-61, 67, 69, 76, 86, 157, 196
Ibn Saud, King	176, 211
Immigration	19, 60, 73, 75, 83, 85, 148, 153, 155, 158, 178, 182-183, 185, 188-189, 191-192, 194, 202-203, 213, 218, 230
Imperial Airways	198
India	93, 193, 207, 213
Industrial development	19, 60, 141, 158, 230
Iraq	84-85, 147, 176, 195, 219
Islington, Lord John	120-121
Israel	16, 56-58, 96, 116, 156, 158, 164, 193, 195, 199-200, 203, 217, 226, 228-229, 236
Italy	33, 42-45, 47, 49-50, 53, 68-70, 75, 228
Jabotinsky, Ze'ev (previously Vladimir)	50-51, 83, 98, 200, 206, 210, 212, 215
Jaffa	18, 93-94, 101, 122, 130-131, 133, 136-137, 139, 154, 162, 164, 166, 172
Jaffa-Jerusalem railway line	93-95
Japanese Military aid	37
Jerusalem	11-12, 17, 59, 73, 85-86, 88, 93, 96, 101, 148, 157, 161-162, 164-165, 175-179, 183, 188, 225
Jerusalem Electric and Public Service Corporation	165
Jewish Agency	159, 178, 180-182, 186, 192, 196-199, 203, 205-206, 208, 214, 217, 219-221, 225-226, 235
Jewish Brigade	47, 49, 52-53, 73, 212
Jewish homeland	27, 43, 47, 69-70, 72, 76, 101, 108, 116, 157-158, 173, 176, 229, 234
Jewish National Fund	79

Jewish Question	56-57
Jewish State	49, 55, 58, 60-61, 80, 115, 206
John Crafton, ship	37
Jordan	77-78, 147, 186, 200-201, 205
Jordan River	11, 17-18, 76-78, 86-87, 89, 92, 96, 101, 105, 109, 117, 133, 139-141, 146-151, 154, 162, 166, 187, 196, 199-200, 208, 230
Joynson-Hicks, Sir	122-124, 126, 128
Kaplan, Fanny	65
Katznelson, Berl	178, 203, 206, 217, 225-227
Keren HaYesod	104
Kerensky, Alexander	55, 61-64, 70, 119, 124, 127, 223
Kineret, Lake	77-78, 129, 144, 199
King David Hotel	225
Kisch, Lt. Colonel Frederick	13, 167, 171-172, 175, 177
Kook, Rabbi Avraham	15, 168-169
Kornilov, General Lavr Georgiyevich	64
Kropotkin, Peter	35
Labour Party	48, 193
Lausanne Treaty	161
League of Nations	76, 83, 87, 115, 118, 120-122, 128, 155, 161-163, 172, 183, 194
Lebanon	72, 78, 141, 195
Lenin, Vladimir	35-36, 46, 63-65, 127, 221-222
Lipsky, Louis	13
Litani River	78, 142, 144
Lloyd George, David	71-72, 74, 81, 122, 142-143, 193
Lloyd, Lord	218-220, 222
Lloyd, T I K	183

London	17, 35-37, 47, 51, 59, 65-66, 72-73, 75, 88-91, 97, 99, 102, 104-105, 107-110, 115, 119, 129-130, 132, 135-136, 142-144, 149, 157, 159, 162, 167-169, 172-173, 175-178, 180-181, 187-189, 193, 195-197, 209, 211-212, 214, 218-219, 221-222, 224, 228, 232
London Conference	209, 212, 214, 218
Luke, Harry	183, 185
Lydda	93, 147, 198
MacDonald, Malcolm	183, 211-213
MacDonald, Ramsay	48-49, 182-183, 187, 189, 191, 193-194
MacMichael, Sir Harold	218, 221
MacPherson, James	237
Magnes, Judah	59, 175-178, 186, 201, 203, 234
Malaria	152
Mandate	73, 75, 87, 109, 115, 117-118, 120, 122-124, 128, 135, 140, 155, 161, 163, 165, 172, 181, 183, 212, 222
Mandatory Authority	104, 208
Mapai Party	216-217
Marshall, Louis	178
Marxism	22, 45
Mavromatis, Euripides	160-165
McMahon-Hussein Correspondence	81
McMahon, Sir Henry	81
Mecca	76
Menashe, Aaron	109
Mesopotamia	72, 81
Milan	45, 51
Military Administration	69, 75, 83
Millerand, Alexandre	142, 144
Molotov-Ribbentrop Pact	223
Mond, Alfred (later Lord Melchett)	109-111, 178, 182, 191
Monte Carlo	36

Morgan-Jones, MP	125
Moscow	24, 65
Mount Carmel	159
Mount Scopus	236
Muslim-Christian Delegation	97, 99
Mussolini, Benito	46, 171, 227-228
Naharayim (Two Rivers)	141, 150, 154-158, 197, 200, 207
Nathan, Harry (later Lord Nathan)	91
Nasatissin, Michael	108
Nashashibi, Rageb	172, 187-188, 211
'National Rejuvenation of the Jewish People'	53
Netanya	236
Nicholas IInd, Tsar	21-24, 29-32, 37-38, 40, 45-46, 52, 62-63
Northcliffe, Lord	115-117
Novomeysky, Moshe	201
New York	15, 52, 59-60, 118, 191
New York Municipality	60
Norfolk	209
Odessa	65-66, 70-71, 88, 127, 143
Okhrana	24, 29, 36, 39-40
Opposition	17, 19, 59-60, 65, 79-80, 86-87, 89, 100-101, 121, 132, 136-138, 147, 155, 161, 166, 177, 188, 190, 197, 201, 231, 235
Orlando, Vittorio Emanuele	74
Ottoman	53, 71
Ozraki	40

Palestine	11-13, 15, 17-20, 22, 27, 34, 43, 45, 47-48, 51, 53, 55-56, 58-62, 68-69, 72-73, 75-78, 80, 82-85, 91, 93-94, 97-99, 104, 107, 109-111, 115-118, 120, 123-125, 128-129, 135-139, 141-148, 151, 154, 157-158, 160-161, 163, 165-168, 172-175, 177-178, 180-181, 183, 185, 187-188, 191-193, 195-196, 198, 200-201, 204-207, 211, 213-214, 216, 218-222, 224-225, 228-229, 231-234
Palestine Airways	198, 229
Palestine Electric Company (previously the Jaffa Electric Company)	109, 136-137, 139, 160, 165, 234
Palestine Railways	94
Palestinian Arab Congress	147
Palestinian Jews	215
Palestinian Nationalism	82, 195
Pan-Arabism	82
Partition Plan	208
Passfield (Lord) (Sidney Webb)	175, 179, 182-184, 186-191, 193, 196, 202
Passfield 'White Paper'	184, 186, 191, 193-194
Passover	159
Peace Conference, Paris	32, 67, 69, 71-72, 80, 125, 142
Peace initiatives	59
Peasant life	20-23, 63, 170
Peel, Lord William Robert	200, 204, 206-208
Peel Report	208
Permanent Court of International Justice	162
Peter and Paul Prison	45, 65
Philby, Colonel H St. John	175-176, 178, 201
Plehve, Vyacheslav	40
Plumer, High Commissioner Field Marshal	147-149
Pogroms	20, 22-23, 44
Politician	146, 160, 166
Politis, His Excellency	154, 162
Preece, Cardew and Rider	95, 130

Pro-Causa Ebraica	44
Putilov iron works	26
Putney Vale Cemetery	65
Rachkovsky, Pyotr	39
Railways	85, 91, 93-96, 220
Ramat Gan	236
Reading, Lord	18, 53, 112, 137-139, 150, 162, 180, 182, 191, 195
Reading Power Station	137-138
'Red Terror'	65
Remez, David	217, 237
Revisionists	200, 206
Revolution, 1905	20, 26, 30, 32-33
Revolution, 1917	17, 20, 33, 55, 58, 61-64, 116, 121, 123, 126, 221
Revolutionary	11, 19-21, 23-25, 27-30, 35-38, 43-44, 48, 54, 62, 64-65, 70, 87, 113, 146, 170, 195, 223, 228-229, 232, 237
Riots	33, 76, 83-84, 89-90, 148, 168-169, 172, 174, 181-183, 185, 192, 207, 213
Rocker, Rudolf	35
Rishon LeTzion	117
Rokach, Israel	217
Romanovs	27
Romny	20
Rothschild, Baron Edouard	108, 184, 196
Rothschild, James de	182
Royal Air Force	199
Russia	11, 20-23, 27, 35-37, 43, 51, 53-55, 58, 61-62, 65, 70, 113, 119, 124, 170, 221, 223, 228, 232
Russian	20-22, 29, 32, 37-38, 45, 51, 53, 55, 60, 65-67, 70, 76, 87, 95, 108, 113, 117-118, 127, 129, 152
Rutenberg Institute	160, 236-237
Rutenberg, Abraham	132, 160
Rutenberg, Anatol	27

Rutenberg, Eugene	27
Rutenberg, Lara	27
Rutenberg, Pinchas	11-18, 20, 24-25, 27-42, 44-511, 53, 57, 59-66, 70-87, 89-100, 103-108, 110-112, 115-133, 135-138, 140-155, 157-161, 163-166, 168-180, 182-189, 191-192, 194-196, 198-223, 225, 228, 232-234, 238
Rutenberg, Piotr	20, 31, 35, 39
Rutenberg, Rochelle	27
Sacher, Harry	132, 172, 179, 195
Safed	175
Salim brothers	199
Samuel, Sir Herbert (later Lord Samuel)	11-12, 18, 72-73, 77, 79, 83-85, 89-90, 94, 97-100, 130, 135, 141, 153, 161, 202
San Remo Conference	83-84
Savinkov, Boris	41
Sde Dov	198
Shaw Report	181, 185, 191
Shofar	168-169
Shertock, Moshe	203
Shuckburgh, Sir John	86, 97-99, 111, 179, 182, 184, 186, 192, 219
Smilansky, Moshe	13, 15, 201, 237-238
Snell, Sir John	94, 182-183, 191
Socialism	20, 23, 46, 55-56, 59, 157, 168
Socialist Revolutionary Party	24, 27, 36, 43, 62, 65, 170
Sokolov, Nahum	72
Solar panels	156
St. Moritz	173
Storrs, Ronald	12-13
St. Petersburg Institute of Technology	21
Sydenham, Lord George	122, 126
Sykes-Picot Agreement	142
Syria	72, 81-85, 195

Taxation	217
Tel Aviv	16-17, 83, 96, 130-131, 133, 136-137, 151, 198, 215, 237
The Daily Mail	116-117
The Times	18, 115-118, 122, 124, 151-154
Tiberias	154
Tiberias-Tzemach road	129
Trade Facilities Commission	110
Trans-Jordan	78, 84-85, 124, 141, 144, 147-149, 176, 185-187, 189, 195, 199-200, 228, 232
Transport and General Workers Union	193
Triple Alliance	47
Trotsky, Leon (Leiba Bronstein)	44, 46, 63-64, 128, 221
Trumpledor, Joseph	51
Turkey	49, 53, 161, 163
Turks	48, 51, 53, 72-73, 75, 81, 93, 123
Ukraine	20
Unemployment	19, 111, 117, 146-147, 153, 158, 230
United Arab Emirates	195
Ushisskin, Menachem	203
Va'ad HaLeumi	146, 168-169, 171-173, 179, 182, 186, 194, 196, 205-206, 211, 215, 217, 224-226, 229, 232-233
Vickers Engineering	87, 94, 136
Vansittart, Sir Robert	142, 144
Vernon, Roland	91, 99
Voith	136
War of independence	156-157
Warburg, Felix	60, 178, 180, 196
Wauchope, Sir Arthur Grenfell	18, 153, 204

Weizmann, Chaim	47-49, 57-60, 72-74, 76, 79-80, 82, 97-98, 103-106, 110, 134, 139, 143, 157, 159, 163, 167, 175, 177-178, 180-183, 186, 188, 191-194, 196-197, 206, 209, 211-214, 230, 233-234
Wilson, Woodrow	53, 71-72, 74
Winter Palace	31-32, 64
Wise, Rabbi Stephen	60
Woodhead, Sir John	208
Woodhead Commission	208
Workers' strike	26, 28, 30, 32-33, 47, 146, 206-207, 213
Wyndam-Deedes, Brigadier-General Wyndam Henry	99
Yarmouk River	144, 151, 156-157
Yeshivat Kerem b'Yavneh	15
Yiddish	15, 21, 52-53
'Yiddisher Congress'	59
Yishuv (Palestinian Jews)	146, 167, 172, 174-175, 196, 199, 203, 205-206, 213-216, 225-226, 229, 233, 235, 237
Yom Kipur	168
'Zion Mule Corps'	51
Zionism	20, 51-52, 59, 115-116, 120, 122, 125, 155, 195, 214
Zionist Congress	98, 178
Zionist Organisation	59-60, 90, 104-106, 119, 163, 167, 171-172, 174, 179-181, 191, 194, 196, 199, 211, 230
Zubatov, Sergeus Vasileyvitch	29

BV - #0054 - 260723 - C41 - 234/156/18 - CC - 9781805140634 - Matt Lamination